Prais
Unburden

"Dr. Catanzaro has provided the field of eating disorders with a long-needed resource addressing the relationship with food in the context of body liberation and through the lens of Internal Family Systems (IFS). As a fat eating disorders and weight discrimination activist with lived experience, I appreciate how I have personally benefited from IFS work and highly recommend this important resource to both clinicians and those pursuing recovery."

—**Chevese Turner,** internationally recognized activist and advocate, CEO of Body Equity Alliance, and founder of the Binge Eating Disorder Association

"With her deep knowledge of Internal Family Systems (IFS) combined with an understanding of anti-diet, weight-inclusive frameworks, Jeanne Catanzaro offers a powerful approach to heal from the disordered eating and body shame that is rampant in our culture. From a place of compassion, Jeanne will show you how dieting, bingeing, self-criticism, and the pursuit of weight loss have been survival strategies, and how you can move toward a more peaceful relationship with food and your body by developing greater curiosity and awareness of your authentic needs. *Unburdened Eating* also serves as an important resource for clinicians to help their clients develop the understanding of 'parts' needed to reconnect with their inner wisdom so that they can trust and nourish their bodies from a place of strength."

—**Judith Matz, LCSW,** coauthor of *The Emotional Eating, Chronic Dieting, Binge Eating & Body Image Workbook* and *Beyond a Shadow of a Diet*

"*Unburdened Eating* is a deeply hopeful book. Jeanne Catanzaro provides a clear, compassionate path to heal your relationship with food and your body. Using the Internal Family Systems approach, you will discover a powerful inner Self, the deepest 'you,' capable of healing the wounds that drive eating disorders, disordered eating, and body shame. This book is an essential guide to gentle and resilient change, and to letting go of the psychological burdens and cultural narratives that impede deep healing. Put this book on the top of your list."

—**Amy Pershing, LMSW, ACSW, CCTP-II,** author of
*Binge Eating Disorder: The Journey to Recovery and
Beyond* and coauthor of *The Emotional Eating, Chronic
Dieting, Binge Eating & Body Image Workbook*

"Do you ever despair of locating inner peace? Jeanne Catanzaro, master IFS therapist and teacher, walks readers through the Internal Family Systems model of mind and therapy, showing us how to take our colonized bodies back, wrest our vision from the eyes of critics, and know that we are loved without having to ask. If you have a body, eat food, and are capable of feeling shame, read this book and help yourself to freedom."

—**Martha Sweezy, PhD,** assistant professor of
psychiatry at Harvard Medical School and author

"*Unburdened Eating* is such a liberating approach to healing from eating disorders and disordered eating. Dr. Jeanne Catanzaro beautifully guides one toward healing in a compassionate and gracious way—ultimately leading to the Self as the ultimate vessel of healing. For anyone who has viewed themselves or their body as "broken," *Unburdened Eating* offers a blueprint on how to honor their body and all of the parts that have served to protect and meet their needs—free from the lens of shame or guilt. This approach can be especially helpful for those from marginalized backgrounds who have experienced trauma and/or have a history of intergenerational trauma, ultimately helping them tap into the embodied, empowered Self."

—**Erikka Taylor, MD, MPH, DFAACAP,** board chair
of Project HEAL, CMO of Arise, and cofounder
of Catalyst Therapeutic Services

"I believe in the power of IFS to help individuals access and heal the wounds that drive their food and body image challenges. This makes *Unburdened Eating* a true gift to anyone who wants to bring this approach into their own life. With deep compassion, Jeanne Catanzaro guides readers with clear steps and relatable anecdotes to help them create a more peaceful relationship with food and their body. I loved reading this book and cannot wait to share it with my clients."

—**Marci Evans, MS, RDN, LDN,** Food and Body Image Healer®

"Jeanne Catanzaro is a gifted clinician with a passion for her subject matter. She has spent most of her career dedicated to breaking the spell of body hatred. *Unburdened Eating* focuses on hope and possibility. This book addresses how through the process of IFS, we can know, understand, and heal beliefs about our relationships to food and our bodies, and explore the ever-present polarizations that society imposes on which bodies are valued and which are not. This is a treasure for clinicians as well as for people interested in exploring new perspectives on their own relationship with eating."

—**Toni Herbine-Blank,** coauthor of *Intimacy from the
Inside Out: Courage and Compassion in Couple Therapy*

Unburdened Eating

Healing Your Relationships
with Food and Your Body
Using an Internal Family
Systems (IFS) Approach

JEANNE CATANZARO, PhD

UNBURDENED EATING

Copyright © 2024 by Jeanne Catanzaro

Published by

Bridge City Books, an imprint of PESI Publishing, Inc.

3839 White Ave

Eau Claire, WI 54703

Illustrations by Sacha Mardou

Cover and interior design by Emily Dyer

Editing by Jenessa Jackson, PhD

Library of Congress Cataloging-in-Publication Data

LCCN: 2024021509

Subjects: LCSH: Eating disorders--Treatment. | Family psychotherapy. | Body image disturbance--Treatment. | Psychic trauma--Treatment. | Self-perception. | Self.

Classification: LCC RC552.E18 C384 2024 | DDC 616.85/26--dc23 /eng/20240520

LC record available at https://lccn.loc.gov/2024021509

ISBN 9781962305204 (print)

ISBN 9781962305211 (ePUB)

ISBN 9781962305228 (ePDF)

All rights reserved.

Printed in the United States of America.

Bridge City Books

Table of Contents

Introduction

If you've picked up this book, you might be a person who thinks a fair amount about your body and how it compares or measures up. You might have been doing this for a long time, since you were young. You might not even remember a time when you didn't worry about your body and what you looked like. Or, if you're like many people, you might recall when that changed, when your intuitive connection to your appetite and your body shifted and you became more self-conscious.

One glaring fact supports your self-consciousness: You live in a culture that tells you your body isn't good enough and that you can and should change it. From the time you are born, you are inundated with messages about your body, how it should look and function, and how you should eat and move to achieve these standards. These beliefs deepen the schism between your mind and body, and you start trying to make it align with what society values: youth, thinness, Whiteness, fitness, health, and able-bodiedness. The pressure to conform is higher if you live in a larger body or if you have the added burdens of bias related to race, gender, class, sexuality, age, or ability. You look for diets or "lifestyle" plans that promise to help you fit in and enter into a painful cycle of being "on" or "off track," depending on what you've eaten, whether you worked out, or what you weighed this morning.

Despite your ample experience that diets and self-criticism don't work, parts of you keep trying one diet or self-improvement plan after another, eliminating certain foods or demonizing parts of your body. When you fail to achieve or sustain your goals, or when you disconnect from your body because it feels like a lost cause, you criticize yourself for not having enough self-discipline. You get more anxious, depressed, or resigned. Again, if you're like a lot of people, it's just a matter of time before parts of you begin looking once again for the diet, cleanse, or wellness plan that will make you feel better about yourself.

Yet, as I tell my friends and clients, it doesn't have to be that way. It is possible to cultivate a more compassionate, or at least a more neutral, relationship with your body. When I tell my friends and clients this, I often hear things like "I hear you, but you might as well be speaking another language. I will never be okay with this body" or "I'm just someone who can't eat carbs" or "I have to do something about this— it's just not healthy to be at this weight." Maybe you can relate. While the prospect of treating your body with more compassion might sound appealing, you likely struggle to sustain this type of relationship with yourself. As much as you try to reject your inner critics and accept your body as it is, parts of you are terrified of what will happen if you stop trying to fix your body, accept yourself *as you are*, and relax into a more compassionate, pleasurable relationship with food and your body.

These fears are well-founded. If you haven't personally experienced stigma related to weight, size, and health, you have most certainly witnessed it all around you. Body shaming, especially regarding fat people, features prominently in news feeds, talk shows, and political commentary. Even if your body aligns well enough at the moment with what's considered "normal," "attractive," and "healthy," deep-seated unconscious judgments against fat people affect all of us. Your memories of being teased as a kid or watching other kids being bullied remain a powerful harbinger of the type of harm that could come your way if you don't keep working hard to fit in. These early memories are reinforced by the judgment and violence you experience or witness as an adult, which lead you to believe that only certain bodies are worthy of praise and protection while others deserve judgment or harm. In turn, you persist in believing there's something wrong with you.

INTRODUCTION

Healing the parts of yourself who are critical or carry shame and fear about food and the body requires an important shift in perspective, one that is central to Unburdened Eating and the Internal Family Systems (IFS) model of psychotherapy upon which it is based. Instead of treating these parts as toxic, IFS encourages you to ask how they have been trying to help you. Even though you may hate these parts for how they make you feel, they are trying to help you survive in a world that judges most bodies as flawed, damaged, or dangerously out of control.

Therefore, rather than trying to get rid of these parts, Unburdened Eating seeks to engage them with compassion and to learn what motivates their behavior. For many people, these parts are driven by early food or body shaming from family, peers, or doctors, and painful or traumatic experiences, especially those related to rejection or stigma. Only when you stop treating these parts as "bad" can you understand their motivations so you can get to the root of the problem—the wounds and vulnerability that your focus on food and the body have attempted to remedy or prevent.

When you attend directly to those hurts, you will no longer need to organize your life around self-improvement. Your critical and diet-minded parts, liberated from their roles, won't continue to look to diet and wellness plans perpetuated by the dominant culture that promise to lift you higher in the "hierarchy of bodies" (Taylor, 2018, p. 64). Instead, you can reconnect with your body and trust it to tell you how much and what kind of nourishment it needs in the way of food, sleep, movement, rest, and companionship. You can finally feel good enough about your body to enjoy a meal, a walk, or a nap without an inner swarm of parts criticizing you.

Indeed, central to the IFS model and to Unburdened Eating is the recognition that we all have an inner wisdom that we can trust to guide us once we are able to get all the competing voices, internal and external, to relax and give space. Each of us is the expert of our own body. With this mindset, you can better appreciate your body for how it is in this moment instead of treating it as a project that either makes you feel hopeless or hopeful—depending on the results of that day's weigh-in or someone else's assessment.

From this perspective, Unburdened Eating provides a systematic way to establish healing relationships with the parts of yourself that have been hurt from living in a culture that pits you against your body's natural appetites and that marginalizes certain bodies. It allows you to become aware of and unburden the painful beliefs and practices that parts of you have adopted in order to fit in or to avoid further harm. As you relate to these limiting strategies with compassion and curiosity, you will learn how to help them transform, causing your choices to be rooted in your core wisdom about what you want and need instead of being driven by external standards.

As your relationships to food and your body transform, so will your relationship to other bodies. You will find that as you release the painful beliefs you've been carrying, you won't be as quick to judge or elevate the people whose bodies align with what you've been taught to dislike or desire. Instead, you will naturally feel more compassion and concern for others.

How This Book Is Organized

This book is organized into seven chapters that introduce you to the key concepts of the IFS model as it applies to your relationships to eating and your body. The chapters build upon each other, so it's best to move through them sequentially. Chapter 1 elaborates how cultural beliefs and practices disrupt your connection to your core wisdom. Chapter 2 introduces the IFS model and provides an overview of its goals and underlying theory. Chapters 3 through 5 describe the steps involved in establishing relationships with your parts, especially those who carry limiting feelings and beliefs or who engage in painful behaviors, so you can heal them and reconnect with your core wisdom.

As you unburden, your relationship to food and your body will increasingly emanate from this inherent wisdom about what you want and need. However, this healing takes time, and even when you've healed the parts of yourself who learned to judge or dislike your body, you'll notice times when they get extreme or become vulnerable to taking on new burdens due to illness, developmental and environmental challenges, and others' judgments. Chapter 6 delineates the components of a Self-Led Eating and Well-Being practice that can help support your continued unburdening and well-being. You'll learn how to negotiate with the parts of yourself who hold different agendas about food and the body on a daily basis, allowing for more ease and collaboration. You'll consider the factors in your own life that impact your ability to make choices that align with your core wisdom and learn ways to help you become less vulnerable to being hurt by others' judgments (e.g., by connecting with communities that support your choice to relate compassionately toward your body). Finally, chapter 7 explores how, as a result of unburdening the toxic beliefs and feelings that parts of you have been made to carry, you can contribute to healing stigma as it manifests in, and is perpetuated by, society at large.

While you'll get a sense of the IFS model by reading this text, this book is not intended as a substitute for training in the IFS model, nor is it a substitute for therapy. Rather, it can be a useful adjunct for those who are already in therapy and a helpful introduction for those who are considering an alternative way to address their eating and body image issues. However, IFS is most easily understood when experienced personally, so I recommend looking into guided IFS meditations online, many of which are available free of charge, as well as on Insight Timer. While these meditations may provide you with some sense of how IFS works, a session with an IFS therapist or practitioner will help you get an idea of the full potential of this respectful, transformative work. I encourage you to consider connecting with a trained professional in your area. To locate an IFS therapist, please visit www.ifs-institute.com and click "Find a Professional."

It is important to note that as a White, straight-sized, cisgender woman with considerable privilege, there is a great deal I don't and can't know about what it's like to live in a body that is subject to ongoing threats of harm and mistreatment. I've learned a great deal from people whose lived experience differs from my own. While I have tried to be inclusive in my thinking and approach, the gaps in my current understanding may lead me to make omissions or mistakes that may be painful for some. I am committed to keep healing my own biases to facilitate my own and others' healing. It is also my hope that you will find in Unburdened Eating a way to contribute to eradicating the interlocking systems that perpetuate so much pain for so many.

A final consideration: This book addresses the impact of painful or traumatic experiences and systemic oppression. You may find it helpful to take breaks and get support from others as you read about this approach to healing. You are the only one who can fully appreciate what you've endured and continue to negotiate in *your* body and in *your* social circles. I invite you to notice your reactions and regard them as meaningful sources of information about how you got hurt, what you had to sacrifice to survive, and what you need to heal.

Chapter 1

Location Is Everything (Where Do You Locate the Problem?)

"Too often people try to change their lives by using the will
as a kind of hammer to beat their life into proper shape.
The intellect identifies the goal of the program, and the will
accordingly forces the life into shape. This way of approaching
the sacredness of one's own presence is externalist and violent.
It brings you falsely outside of yourself and you can spend
years lost in the wilderness of your own mechanical, spiritual
programs. You can perish in a famine of your own making."

–John O'Donohue

Take a few moments to notice the different thoughts and feelings that emerge as you reflect on these words. If you're someone who's been dedicated to changing your body via diets, wellness, and fitness programs, or if you spend a lot of time shaming yourself for not doing these things, you may notice that you relate to the pain of wanting, and not being able, to lose weight or change your body.

If you're dominated by shame, you may not question or even notice the inference that your preoccupation with fixing yourself is a "famine of your own making." You may not realize how your relationships with food and your body have been shaped by the dominant culture's most deeply held values. If you've found yourself thinking "where there's a will, there's a way," or "no pain, no gain," parts of you have taken on some of these beliefs. These ideas are so widely held and communicated by family members, friends, doctors, teachers, and politicians that you often do not even notice or question them.

Until you understand the deeper motivations that keep you trying to shrink or otherwise change your body (and even when you do know), parts of you will keep trying because they believe something is wrong with you when you either can't do something or don't want to. That's because these parts learned as children that certain bodies are worthy of praise and protection while others deserve judgment or harm. That thin, White, fit, cisgender, heterosexual bodies are most desirable while Black, disabled, and fat bodies, among others, are subject to discrimination and negative stereotypes—most commonly that these people are lazy and indulgent.

Since fatness is seen as pathological and something you can and should change as opposed to a natural variation in body type, bias against fat people is sanctioned in the dominant culture. If you haven't been teased for your body size or what you weigh, you have witnessed how badly fat people are treated. Parts of you become determined to either lose weight or avoid gaining weight.

Again, pause for a few moments and see what thoughts and feelings arise as you take in this information. How often do you find yourself worrying about gaining weight or looking the way you "should"? How often do you attribute your struggles to not having enough self-control? Given the way discipline and willpower are seen as virtues that one cultivates, it would be surprising if you didn't.

The importance of willpower as a core American value is reflected in the considerable amount of attention dedicated to understanding this subject. A well-known series of studies, colloquially known as the "marshmallow test," assessed preschoolers' ability to tolerate holding off on eating a single marshmallow or some other treat in anticipation of a larger payoff if they could delay gratification (Mischel & Ebbesen, 1970; Mischel et al., 1972). The children were given a treat and told they would receive a larger amount or a more preferable treat if they could wait to eat it until the experimenter returned to the room. If they didn't want to wait, they could signal the experimenter and immediately get the single, but less preferred, treat. Follow-up studies reported that kids who were able to delay gratification were more likely to do well later in life in a number of areas the dominant culture commonly associates with success, like higher SAT scores and greater frustration tolerance in adolescence (Shoda et al., 1990) as well as lower body mass index (BMI) in adulthood (Schlam, et al., 2013).

More recent replications of the marshmallow test have included samples that are more diverse than those in the original studies (e.g., Kidd et al., 2013; Watts et al., 2018). Kidd and colleagues (2013) also manipulated the experimenter's reliability as a factor; some children were led to believe that the experimenter could be trusted while others were led to believe that the experimenter could not be trusted to follow through on their word. Not surprisingly, this study found that children who doubted the reliability of the experimenter were much more likely to eat the first treat instead of delaying gratification for a second treat. Although the children's behavior could be construed as impulsive, it actually makes sense given their environment. When children didn't trust the adult in the room to take care of them, they acted in ways to take care of themselves. Their behavior was at least, in part, an adaptation to the expectation of unreliable circumstances. Why not take the single marshmallow if waiting for the second would leave you potentially empty-handed? This research aligns with some of Mischel's earliest observations on delay of gratification (e.g., Mischel, 1961; Mischel & Grusec, 1967).

This kind of perspective, one that highlights the social context that frames our choices, is more of an exception in the dominant culture, which largely ignores or pays lip service to how factors like stress, poverty, stigma, food insecurity, and class privilege impact individual behavior and well-being. Almost sixty years later, the interest in self-control as an individual trait rooted in willpower is holding steady. Controlling one's appetites is seen as the key to success in many different spheres—financial, social, health, and so forth. As researcher David DeSteno (2014) has observed, "As the capacity to delay gratification seems more and more like destiny, we are becoming a culture obsessed with self-regulation"—so obsessed, he noted, that even *Sesame Street*'s Cookie Monster has been taught to employ various cognitive strategies to suppress his desire for more cookies.

Maybe it is time to ask yourself if repressing your desire for cookies is the only way to approach how you eat and how you view your body. Perhaps the fact that you are reading this book means you already know there has to be a better way.

How All of This Relates to You

At this point, you may find yourself saying things like "C'mon, I just want to be healthy" or "This sounds good, but I need to lose ten or fifteen pounds to feel more comfortable (e.g., in my body, in my clothes)." You may find that you don't want to think about the larger picture—how the dominant culture treats bodies (e.g., "What does this have to do with White supremacy or racism? Everyone knows being fat is unhealthy!").

Here's something to consider: The blame, lack of compassion, and suffering you observe at the societal level also play out *internally*. The parts of you who work to align with what those around you value—your family, friends, community, ethnic group, larger culture—try to fix the aspects of yourself that are considered unacceptable or less desirable. In essence, they act like the unreliable experimenter in the marshmallow studies, withholding what you really want or need. These parts of you shame or judge you for being "impulsive" or lacking self-control when other parts act to satisfy those unmet needs. Over time, you feel increasingly chaotic as these different parts fight with each other.

How Unburdened Eating Can Help

Living in and taking care of a human body is challenging. Much of the time, when you check inside, you'll notice competing, and often conflicting, wants and needs. While one part of you wants to go for a walk, for example, another part of you—one who is stressed about all of the work you have to do—pushes to keep working. When these different impulses aren't motivated by shame and fear (e.g., "I have to go for a walk because I'll hear it from my [mother, doctor, partner] if I don't lose weight"), you can simply check in with what feels right in that moment.

Yet for many of us, simply "checking in" with ourselves doesn't lead to a simple answer. It's too loud in there! Burdened as you are by so many beliefs about food and your body, the decisions you make about what you should eat, how you should move, and how you should look are fraught with fear, confusion, and shame. The competing thoughts and feelings drown out, or make it hard to stay clear about, your own wisdom about what you and your body need. Your conviction that there's something inherently wrong with you for being so conflicted or out of control deepens. Since you blame yourself for this, you try to control the parts who eat "too much" or who don't exercise enough—or you try to silence your inner critic.

When you can get curious about the different beliefs and feelings you have about food and your body and how they impact you, things start to look a lot different. This is what Richard Schwartz (1995) found as a result of his early work with clients with eating disorders. Schwartz observed how his clients' seemingly chaotic—and, often, extreme— thoughts, feelings, and behaviors didn't seem so extreme when he could get them to focus on them, one at a time, with some amount of curiosity and openness. As his clients reflected on their inner experiences from this nonjudgmental place, they discovered these thoughts, feelings, and behaviors were emanating from *parts*, or sub personalities, of themselves who had distinct roles in their systems.

You'll learn a lot more about parts as you read on. For the moment, what's important to know is that it's natural and useful to have multiple parts within yourself. You may find it helpful to think of parts as inner children, each with a range of feelings, preferences, perspectives, and agendas. Like real children, parts differ in their temperaments, their ages, and the ways they manifest emotionally and physically. For example, the part of you who loves to sing fills your chest with excited energy when someone mentions karaoke. In contrast, a part who shames you for what you look like may speak harshly, in a parental tone, causing another part to register its shame with a quick flash of heat across your chest and face. Like kids in a family, some parts get along, or form alliances, and others fight with each other. As you get to know your parts, you'll start to recognize and even anticipate these inner dynamics.

When Schwartz's clients got curious about their parts, they learned that their feelings and actions made sense given their histories and the current contexts of their lives. For example, some clients who had bingeing parts discovered that this behavior had helped them feel more grounded when they were left alone as children in unstable or abusive families. Other clients described how the parts who got them to purge helped the clients feel sleepy, which alleviated their intense anxiety. Once the clients understood their parts' intentions, their relationships with these parts transformed. Behaviors they'd disliked or feared because they seemed so self-destructive or limiting were now seen as important coping strategies.

As they continued to focus on their inner experiences from a place of curiosity, the clients described feeling more open and having more compassion for the different parts of themselves. They related that, in this state, they felt more like their true selves. Schwartz came to call this state of being the *Self*.

The Self

The Self is the calm, spacious energy that spontaneously emerges when you mentally separate, or *unblend*, from parts so you aren't dominated by their thoughts, feelings, images, memories, and sensations. (Unblending is a process that you'll learn more about in chapter 3.) The Self is an internal resource that exists within each of us, separate from our parts. It functions like a wise and caring parent, supporting the needs of individual parts and helping to negotiate conflicts between them so the system runs smoothly. The concept of an inner healing wisdom is common to many religious and spiritual traditions. You may be familiar with the higher powers central to Christian religions, as well as twelve-step recovery programs. It's also the essence Sonya Renee Taylor (2018) seems to describe with her concept of radical self-love.

Unlike parts, the Self isn't charged with feelings like overwhelm or anger. It isn't driven by needs or agendas like losing weight or avoiding criticism. Instead, it holds the desire for growth and healing at all system levels: individuals, groups, and the larger culture. This book will help you clarify what the Self is and help you to know when you're in that state versus when you're dominated by the thoughts and feelings of one or more of your parts. For now, the place to begin is also the simplest to understand. Being Self-led (or "in Self") feels good. When you're led by the Self, you will notice feeling a kind of calm, open, alive, or grounded energy. While your personal experience with Self-energy may differ from someone else's—for example, you may feel more energized versus calm—it will typically comprise some combination of the qualities that IFS refers to as the 8 Cs: calm, curiosity, courage, compassion, connectedness, clarity, confidence, and creativity.

Qualities of Self:
The 8 Cs

How Parts Relate to the Self

The IFS model holds that each of us comes into the world with parts who, in ideal circumstances, emerge at developmentally appropriate times to assist in our functioning. Most of these parts exist naturally in a state of flow, unencumbered by fear, shame, or limiting beliefs. If you've noticed young kids posing for selfies, dancing, or eating with abandon, you've witnessed unburdened parts in action. While the Self may need to intervene and negotiate with these parts when their wants and needs conflict, on the whole, unburdened parts coexist with relative ease.

Ideally, our parts would continue in this unfettered state. Many of them do. For example, you probably don't think much about the part of you who loves music or the part who loves to read. However, when you inevitably get hurt by people or endure upsetting or traumatic events, some parts take on extreme beliefs and feelings about themselves and the world. IFS refers to these beliefs and feelings as *burdens*.

Defined as "the extreme ideas and feeling states that accrue from frightening or shaming interactions or events that parts carry on or in their bodies" (Schwartz & Sweezy, 2020, p. 281), burdens are a fundamental aspect of the human experience. However, while we all get burdened, we differ in terms of the number and extremity of the burdens we carry. The extent to which we must work to align with the values of our respective cultures—our families, our ethnic groups, the dominant culture at large—correlates with how burdened each of us is likely to be.

The relationship between parts and burdens is akin to a person with a virus. Recall a time when you've had a cold or the flu. The virus may have made you feel not quite like yourself, or even like you couldn't function. However, once the virus left your body, you could go back to your usual way of operating. This is similar to what happens when parts of you take on burdens. They feel and act in extreme ways. Stuck in the past *at the time when they got hurt*, these parts need help from the Self to cast off their burdens so they can revert back to their naturally valuable, non-extreme states.

Healing Burdens: The Key to Reconnecting with Your Core Wisdom

Unburdened Eating offers a way to release the extreme feelings and beliefs you've taken on about food and your body so you can reconnect with what you, at your core, know you need. As this happens, your decisions about food, movement, rest, and pleasure increasingly emanate from this core wisdom, which IFS calls the Self. While you may believe all of the dieting and trauma you've experienced have irreparably damaged your inherent healing essence, or that you never possessed this wisdom, the good news is that the Self is in each of us and *cannot be damaged* by trauma. Like the sun, it is always there: it is not diminished by the clouds (i.e., burdened parts) that cover it, nor is it made bigger when the clouds lift (i.e., when parts unblend), even though it may seem that way.

The Self reemerges as parts are helped to separate, or unblend, so they can be witnessed for the pain they've endured and helped to release the toxic beliefs and feelings they were made to carry. Once you heal the parts who learned to dislike or hate your body, or to view it as a way to elicit praise and avoid rejection, you'll notice more ease and collaboration between and among your parts because how you look and what you eat are no longer urgent matters. When you do notice the old critical or diet-minded parts coming up again, you'll trust that this a sign that some part of you needs your attention, and you will respond to that need instead of letting the critical or diet-minded part bully you into the latest boot camp or detox. Finally, you'll become more Self-protective in the external world, spending time with people and in spaces that are respectful, relying on your core wisdom to let you know when you need to set limits or establish boundaries.

But First, the Basics

While Unburdened Eating may sound good on an intellectual level, you may also notice that you have a lot of skepticism or concern. You may believe that even if Unburdened Eating helps some people, it won't work for you. You may believe that your inner critic won't budge or that the part who worries about your health will remain steadfast in its pursuit of weight loss. You may notice parts who worry that Unburdened Eating will just be another set of rules to follow. Other parts may fear you will end up feeling out of control or hurt by people when they see you accepting or even enjoying your body as it is. If you're already planning how this won't work for you, I invite you to get curious.

One of the basic tenets of IFS you'll learn about is the principle that "all parts are welcome" in your system. Even when what they do doesn't make you feel great, or when they act in extreme or seemingly destructive ways, each of your parts has a positive intention. If you can be curious about the reactions you're having, you'll find out more about how to help the parts of yourself who have been stuck in painful relationships with food and your body. To help you develop this new way of relating to yourself, the next chapter will elaborate on the basic components and principles of the IFS model.

Chapter 2

A New Way of Relating to Yourself

"We did not start life in a negative partnership with our bodies.
I have never seen a toddler lament the size of their thighs,
the squishiness of their bellies. Children do not arrive here
ashamed of their race, gender, age, or disabilities."

–Sonya Renee Taylor

One of my clients, Mara, was a lot like many of the women I know and meet with in my clinical practice. In her initial session, she described a long history of "disordered" eating. It was hard for her to remember a time when she enjoyed food without feeling guilty or engaging in some calculation—how what she ate would impact how much she ate later in the day or the next day, or how much time she spent at the gym. Desperate to lose weight, she was also tired of worrying about what she looked like and what she weighed.

In describing her experience with dieting, Mara explained, "I lose some weight and that feels good. But then I start adding things here and there, and before I know it, I'm back where I was."

While Mara felt drawn to Intuitive Eating (Tribole & Resch, 2020), she found that it left her feeling rudderless. "I'm just someone who needs structure. I'm the type who checks in with how I'm feeling and I'm always a bit hungry. I can always eat something. So I do. And then

I notice my weight going up, and that makes me feel like *Fuck it, I'm never going to get this right.*"

Since Mara had looked for so long to diets and wellness plans to tell her what to eat and how to move, she became more confused about what felt right for her and what was "good" for her. She believed she needed to be vigilant or else she'd lose control of her eating and keep gaining weight. "I don't get anywhere unless I have clear rules," she told me.

Mara felt there was something wrong with her because she felt so chaotic and her eating and exercise practices were inconsistent. She was particularly upset about her habit of eating at night. She could plan and make time to prepare something healthy for dinner, but then she'd end up eating a sleeve of cookies while watching TV.

"There's no good reason for that," she told me. "Even when I like what I've eaten for dinner, I get this idea that I'll just have a couple of cookies after. Before I know it, I've eaten half the box."

Mara berated herself for sabotaging her weight loss efforts at night. "I don't know why I keep doing the same thing and expecting a different outcome," she said, referring to how she kept cookies and ice cream in the house. "I know they're always trouble for me, so it makes no sense. It's stupid, really."

However, when she thought of not having these treats around, she noticed this didn't feel right to her either. "I want to be the type of person who can have this stuff around and just have it in moderation."

When I asked Mara if she was curious about why she was eating at night, she rolled her eyes.

"I've thought *a lot* about why I do what I do. I know I'm lonely at night, I should just read a book or something and not eat. Have a cup of tea. But I always end up eating something, and that's what's getting in the way. That's why I will never lose weight."

"I hear how frustrated you are. Has criticizing yourself been helpful with the eating at night?" I asked, risking another eye roll.

"Nope, I can't say it has. At least not now. It *has* worked in the past, but not now. But I've also tried *not* beating myself up, and that hasn't worked either."

"I'm going to propose we try something different today and see if it feels more helpful."

Mara was quiet.

I continued, saying, "I'm wondering if we can get to know the part of you who is so angry with you for eating at night."

"I'm not sure what there is to say. I eat food I shouldn't eat and I eat more than I should. It's frustrating."

"Do you know why this part of you is so concerned about losing weight? What does it believe is at stake if you don't lose weight?"

"I look terrible, to start with. I can't find anything to wear, and I refuse to buy a whole new wardrobe. I don't know how I'm going to possibly meet someone looking like this. And then I'm like *Fuck it. Do I really want to be with someone if I have to work so hard to look a certain way for them?* I am so sick of worrying about this."

I said, "So a part of you is totally focused on weight loss and another part is really tired of worrying about it."

"Yes, it's exhausting. I really don't want to waste more of my life like this. It makes me really sad and also a little pathetic when I think about how much time I've spent obsessing about my body. But I can't seem to stop. I have so many different thoughts and feelings about it, but I don't think it needs to be so complicated. If I could just make a plan that works and stick with it."

Mara's instinct that she needed some structure was correct. However, instead of a set of rules telling her what to do, what she needed was a different way to relate to the "mess" of thoughts and feelings she had about food and her body that made it so difficult for her to know what she wanted and needed.

Listening carefully to Mara's description of her difficulties, I noted what seemed like different voices engaging in a heated debate. The one who pushed Mara to lose weight was sharp and frustrated, while the one who wanted her to stop obsessing sounded weary and also shaming about all the time she'd "wasted." Sadness and anxiety emerged here and there, especially when Mara spoke about dating and her concerns about being rejected because of her size.

Like many people, Mara tended to judge her thoughts, feelings, and behaviors for being extreme and, often, contradictory. She spent a fair amount of time trying to change the different aspects of her internal experience. I knew that if Mara could instead get curious about these parts of herself, she'd see them in a new light. They'd make more sense to her and she'd be able to help them become less extreme.

When I suggested this to Mara, she interrupted me to say, "Yes, but I already do this. I ask myself why I want to eat. I know it's because I'm feeling lonely or tired. I tell myself it's not going to make me feel better afterward, and then I do it anyway."

I responded, "I understand that you've thought a lot about this pattern of nighttime eating and that being aware and thinking about it hasn't stopped it from happening. Neither has judging it or trying to control it. If you're open to it, I can show you that there's a different way to relate to the part who gets you to eat at night. Even if it doesn't seem like it, this part, like each of your parts, has a protective or positive intention that motivates it to do what it does. If you can get curious about it, it will tell you why it feels and behaves the way it does. But first we need to get the parts of you who are frustrated with the nighttime-eating part to give you some room so you can get to know it better."

Mara contemplated this new information before saying, "I don't know how I can be genuinely curious about something I find so frustrating and that causes me so much pain."

"Of course. The parts of you who are frustrated have good reason to be. So let them know you understand that. But also let them know that if they relax a bit, we can get to know more about the part who eats and what drives it to do that. Then we can help it so it doesn't need to keep doing that. See if they're willing to try."

Mara shrugged. "I'll try, but I'm not sure I understand what you mean by 'get them to relax back.'"

"That makes sense. This is a shift in how you usually relate to yourself. Do you notice where you sense the frustration? Focus your attention on those parts and let them know that you are listening to them. Do their concerns make sense to you?"

"Yes, they do."

When Mara validated the frustrated parts of herself, they relaxed a bit. She noticed feeling less agitated and also more curious. In IFS terms, Mara had more access to her core wisdom, or Self, as the parts who were frustrated with the nighttime-eating part were able to *unblend*, or separate, a bit from her. As a result, she could learn more about the extreme feelings and beliefs (burdens) and other things (e.g., hunger, boredom, fatigue) that motivated part of her to eat at night.

Burdens: The Root of the Problem

As you learned in the last chapter, burdens are the feelings and beliefs that attach to parts of you and cause them to feel and behave in extreme ways. IFS differentiates between three kinds of burdens: personal burdens, legacy burdens, and cultural burdens. *Personal burdens* are extreme feelings, energies, and beliefs that enter our systems from our direct, or lived, experience. These experiences include overwhelming or traumatic events, as well as more subtle experiences, including neglect and other attachment traumas or injuries. For example, when Mara was a child, she was shamed by her pediatrician for gaining "too much" weight during puberty, causing vulnerable parts in her system to feel humiliated. This shame was compounded by teasing from her classmates, who noticed and made fun of her for developing early.

The likelihood that a given event will be burdening depends on a number of factors, including how vulnerable the individual's system is already. The more parts there are who feel worthless, scared, or ashamed, the less Self-energy there is to handle a given stressor. Also, as you'll hear a lot about throughout this book, the degree to which people in the external environment are burdened also influences how damaging a particular event will be. Mara's painful experience with her pediatrician and the kids at school came on the heels of her family's abrupt move to a less affluent town when her father got laid off and had a hard time finding work. Neither of her parents had the emotional bandwidth to help her with the distress she felt about these transitions.

As a young girl, Mara didn't question her doctor's harsh assessment, not only because he was an authority figure, but because parts of her had already absorbed her family's anti-fat bias. These anti-fat attitudes reflect the second type of burdens in IFS known as *legacy burdens*, or the "intergenerational transmission of constraining, negative feelings and beliefs" (Sinko, 2016, p. 164). Legacy burdens differ from personal burdens in that they are transmitted from others rather than being the result of personal experience. For example, Mara's mother had grown up with a father who prized self-discipline and scrutinized all of his children, especially his daughters, for what they looked like. As a result, Mara's mother was always trying to figure out what she could wear to minimize her "problem areas." From the time Mara was a little girl, she observed her mother's dissatisfaction with her own body. While Mara's father was more relaxed with regard to food and most things, he and his sister had struggled with their weight since they were young. He became concerned when he noticed Mara putting on weight as she entered adolescence.

Had either of Mara's parents soothed her during or after her appointment with the pediatrician, or if they had challenged the doctor's assessment, they might have mitigated the harm of the doctor's feedback. However, because they carried legacy burdens related to body size, health, and authority, they responded to the pediatrician's feedback by putting Mara on a diet, the first of several she tried as a teenager.

Even if Mara had experienced the good fortune of growing up in a family that didn't transmit many legacy burdens related to weight and the body, she would still have had to contend with *cultural legacy burdens*. When it comes to health and appearance, the dominant culture reinforces the idea that weight gain, especially among women's bodies, is unattractive, unhealthy, and to be avoided at all costs. Therefore, the pediatrician's response to Mara's pubertal weight gain reflects the cultural legacy burden of anti-fat bias. As a teenager, Mara was particularly vulnerable to the doctor's assessment because of what she saw on TV, in magazines, and at school.

She explained, "I wanted to look like the most popular girls in my class. They were wealthy, thin, blonde, and had straight hair. I wasn't very tall and I was curvy. It took me years to understand that what I wanted wasn't physically possible."

What Mara didn't realize—and had struggled to come to terms with—was that her parts were carrying burdens rooted in longstanding cultural prejudice stemming from White supremacy and classism. She believed that if she just worked harder and exerted more self-control, she would have the thin, healthy, attractive body that she coveted and that is celebrated by the dominant culture.

If, like Mara, you've grown up or spent much time in Western culture, parts of you have undoubtedly absorbed the dominant culture's ideas about which bodies are the most esteemed for how they look and function. You may not notice or question these beliefs because you've held them for so long, and they're perpetuated in so many ways by the people and institutions around you. However, they are nonetheless present and affect the way you see and relate to your own and other people's bodies.

You'll learn a lot about burdens in this book because they disconnect you from your core wisdom and make parts of you feel and act in extreme ways. When parts of you take on burdens about food, for example, they no longer trust your Self to determine what you and your body need. Instead of checking in with yourself, burdened parts rely on the latest diet or health guru to tell them what to do. They lead you to compare yourself to others, which can leave you feeling better or worse, depending on whom you're comparing yourself to.

Burdened Parts and Their Different Roles

As you've learned, when parts get burdened, they become extreme in how they feel and how they act. In this capacity, burdened parts can take on two different types of roles in the inner system: exiles or protectors (managers and firefighters).

Exiles

When you experience stressful or traumatic events, parts of you can get injured and carry the pain, fear, or shame related to those experiences. These parts are known as *exiles*, and they make sense of the trauma that's happened by taking on negative beliefs about themselves and the world. For example, when Mara was criticized by her parents for wanting more to eat, a young part of her came to believe that there was something wrong with her for wanting more food. This part felt shame about her appetite for food and a lot of other things.

Exiles are literally exiled by other protective parts of the system who fear that the exiles' burdens are too painful for you to bear or will leave you vulnerable to more wounding from the outside. To exile a part, protectors (who you'll learn about in a moment) split it off from your awareness, freezing this part in time at the age at which it experienced the stressful or traumatic event. This is one reason why you may remember so vividly the time in first grade when your friend made fun of you for wearing pants that were too short. Isolated from the rest of the system, your exiles don't know that you are an adult who can

20

now tolerate such criticism or take care to avoid people who are likely to perpetrate it.

Another reason why exiles are commonly shunned is because they possess qualities that are upsetting to family or other people. A good example is an emotionally sensitive child who grows up in a family that avoids feelings. The child's sensitivity is a liability in such a family. As a result, the child comes to exile their intuitive parts through the action of protective parts. This allows the child to shut off their awareness of things that, if they gave voice to them, would likely invite some kind of put-down, dismissal, or worse from their parents. Some exiles who don't carry burdens get suppressed because their joy, playfulness, intelligence, confidence, or other qualities would somehow upset the family or cultural group.

Protectors

Protectors are parts of the system who adopt any number of strategies to keep you from feeling pain or vulnerability. They don't choose their roles but are forced to take them on by the circumstances in which they find themselves, much like parentified children. Protectors work to shield you from emotional pain in two ways: by keeping exiles out of your awareness and by avoiding situations that could either activate the exiles or expose them to further harm. The protector who tells you to "get over it, it's not so bad" is trying to shove aside young parts who still hold shame or fear. It does this to protect you from experiencing the pain of those feelings and to prevent you from getting mocked by others who are intolerant of or might exploit the exiles' shame and fear.

If, like Mara, you were shamed for wanting more food—either because someone disapproved of how much you ate or felt stressed because there wasn't enough food in the house—you may notice a protector who gives the message that there's something wrong with you for wanting more. This activates other protectors to do what they can to suppress your hungry parts so you don't risk being shamed further and so you don't feel the exiles' deprivation.

Protectors fall into one of two groups: *managers* and *firefighters*. While they may use the same behaviors, the key difference between the two types of protectors is whether they're proactive or reactive in executing their strategies. Managers are proactive, steadily doing what they can to make sure you don't feel the exiles' vulnerability and so they don't get hurt again. For example, a part who is constantly occupied with "clean" eating may be a manager working to stave off an exile's terror. The planning and preparation involved in eating every color of the rainbow every day prevents you from feeling very much; it may also elicit others' admiration, which helps to buffer the well of exiled pain. In contrast to managers, firefighters are reactive, springing into action once exiles break through to your awareness, which they inevitably will at some point. The part who suddenly adopts a plan to eat "clean" on the heels of a breakup is likely a firefighter doing its best to provide relief from the surge of exiled terror that ensues. Focusing on gathering all the "right" foods can distract you, at least temporarily, from the exile's misery.

As you make your way through this book, you'll likely discover some of the ways your protectors have been trying to take care of you. You'll also learn how you can negotiate with your protectors so they trust you enough to let go of their strategies and let you handle things. First, however, let's learn more about the different types of protectors.

Managers

Managers are the parts of you who work hard to make you look good, who try to hide or control anything that might result in you being judged, blamed, shamed, or hurt. They are often future-oriented and strategic in nature (e.g., "Do/don't do that or else ____ will happen").

Mara's critical part is a good example of a manager—one you can probably relate to. It warned her about all the things that could happen if she didn't lose weight or continued to gain weight. You'll likely recognize some of your other managers in the following table.

Common Manager Roles	
Controllers	Producers/Achievers
Intellectualizers/Analyzers	Caretakers
Restrictors	People pleasers
Perfectionists	Minimizers/Suppressors
Avoiders	Planners

As you'll learn more about in the next chapter, since managers are valued in the dominant culture, many people identify with these parts so much that they don't recognize they are managers. For example, Mara's critical part was such a commanding presence in her internal system, and so similar to parts she observed among her family and friends, that she had a hard time believing this manager was a part of her and not "just who I am."

A quick check inside clarified this for her. When Mara's critical manager was around, she didn't sense any of the qualities of Self (the 8 Cs). Instead, she felt tension in her neck and shoulders and also heard a harsh voice that threatened, "You'd better lose this weight or else!"

Although managers are commonly the first line of defense against painful or overwhelming feelings, when their efforts fall short and something activates exiles' feelings of worthlessness, shame, or fear, the second type of protectors—firefighters—come to the rescue.

Firefighters

Like actual firefighters, these protective parts react to the emergency of emotional pain with quick, and often extreme, actions designed to snuff out the exiles' pain. Unlike managers, firefighters are focused on bringing immediate relief. They don't consider the cost or future consequences of their actions. Firefighters use any number of strategies to escape the "fire" of the exiles' distress. Common firefighter strategies include distracting, lashing out, restricting, purging, dissociating, and using alcohol, food, and various substances to disconnect from the feelings.

Mara's peanut–butter seeking part is a good example of a firefighter. Whenever Mara's mother got angry with her and stopped talking to her, a firefighter rushed in to block out Mara's ensuing panic by eating peanut butter. As the firefighter binged on peanut butter, it disconnected Mara from the exile who became so scared by her mother's stonewalling. Instead of feeling panicked and uncertain, Mara felt soothed by the peanut butter's taste and texture. It had an almost hypnotic effect as she repeatedly spooned it from the jar. For a few moments, as Mara's firefighter narrowed her attention to focus only on the peanut butter, she felt relieved.

Whereas Mara's manager considered the consequences of eating or bingeing on peanut butter (e.g., "You'll get fat," "You'll ruin your diet"), her firefighter had no such concerns. Its single focus was to help her feel better. You may relate to this part of Mara or some of the other common firefighter activities listed here.

Common Firefighter Roles	
Distractors/Soothers (via substances, activities, food)	Deflectors (via sarcasm, humor)
Attackers (physical, emotional) of oneself or others	Adventurers/Pleasure seekers
Dissociators	Rule breakers

Inasmuch as firefighters don't care about the consequences of their actions, they tend to be viewed negatively by managers—both your own and those of the people around you—who are quite concerned with appearances and good behavior. Thus, for Mara, the relief afforded by the peanut butter was short-lived, as her critical manager quickly interjected, "This is why you will never lose weight!" In that moment, all the manager could think about was how to get the peanut–butter seeking firefighter to stop. In its mind, the peanut butter was a huge problem. If Mara gained weight, she would have a harder time attracting a partner. She would also hear it from her mother, who always commented on Mara's weight. Her manager grabbed the peanut butter and put it out of reach.

These disagreements between parts regarding how to best take care of the system are called polarizations, which we'll take a deeper look at next.

Polarizations

As you've learned, protectors adopt any number of strategies to take care of the internal system. Each is quite opinionated about its approach, believing it to be the best way to handle things. When one protector (or group of protectors) gets extreme, other protectors (or groups of protectors) act in opposite or competing ways to balance out the system.

The concept of polarizations will resonate with you if you've ever dieted for a period of time. As your diet-minded managers eliminate food, you feel increasingly deprived, which motivates your firefighters to ease the hunger and dissatisfaction. Since your managers fear this behavior will sabotage their health or weight-loss goals, they become even more restrictive, which only makes you hungrier, so you eat more and often end up bingeing.

This example illustrates how polarizations escalate over time. As polarized parts persist in their respective strategies, they typically become more distrustful of each other and, as a result, more extreme. They also impact all parts of the system. For example, when Mara's manager scolded her firefighter for eating peanut butter, it amplified her exiles' shame. This fueled the firefighter's determination to distract Mara from the exiles' painful feelings. Ignoring the critic's rebuke, the firefighter climbed onto the counter to find the peanut butter the manager had hidden in the farthest corner of the pantry.

While you'll commonly find managers battling with firefighters, it's also common to have multiple managers whose strategies conflict or a number of firefighters who have different ideas about how to protect the system. An example of polarized firefighters is when one firefighter is about to lash out and a second firefighter shuts everything down so your mind goes "blank." Polarizations also occur between exiles and protectors. For example, because Mara's parents had little tolerance for her anxiety, a manager in her system hated her exiles for their "weakness." The more anxious they were, the more contemptuous her critical manager became.

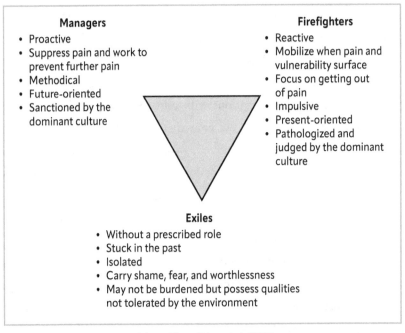

Managers
- Proactive
- Suppress pain and work to prevent further pain
- Methodical
- Future-oriented
- Sanctioned by the dominant culture

Firefighters
- Reactive
- Mobilize when pain and vulnerability surface
- Focus on getting out of pain
- Impulsive
- Present-oriented
- Pathologized and judged by the dominant culture

Exiles
- Without a prescribed role
- Stuck in the past
- Isolated
- Carry shame, fear, and worthlessness
- May not be burdened but possess qualities not tolerated by the environment

Adapted from Sykes et al. (2023)

Polarizations are ubiquitous, occurring at all levels of systems, between and within governments or racial groups, partners in a couple, and parts within yourself. You can learn about polarizations in more detail in *Internal Family Systems for Addictions* (Sykes et al., 2023). For now, Mara's experience illustrates how polarizations develop in the internal system.

Mara was solidly stuck in a battle between the parts of herself who were sick and tired of dieting and the parts of herself who were committed to changing her body. Since she was dominated most often by the critical part who scolded her for eating and told her she needed to lose weight, I suggested we start by getting to know more about that part.

Her response was unsurprising. "That part is right. I do need to lose weight. I really think if I could just lose a little weight, it would relax a little."

I replied, "So a part of you agrees with the critical part who tells you you're not okay, that you need to lose weight."

"Yeah, I think pretty much all of me agrees with it, even though I hate feeling that way."

"Right, so even though some parts of you hate feeling the criticism, many other parts feel like it's necessary."

Mara nodded.

Here, Mara confirmed that she was blended with parts who allied with the critical part. When parts blend, you see, hear, feel, and experience things the way they do. But trying to get to know one part when you're blended with another isn't helpful for a couple of reasons. Imagine you're at a party and you meet someone new. As you introduce yourself and express interest in getting to know this person, someone else cuts in between you. This new person blocks your access to the first person and if you persist in trying to learn more about them, any information you get will reflect the opinion of the part who's interrupted.

"Mara, I'm wondering if you can focus your attention inside and ask all the parts who have opinions about the critical part—both positive and negative—to give you some space so you can get to know the critic better. Let them know that if they agree to give you some room, you'll be able to learn a bit more about what the critic has been trying to do for you."

Mara closed her eyes to focus inside. After a few moments, she nodded and, with her eyes still closed, replied, "Okay. I'm a little more open."

I responded, "Okay. Now see if you can notice how this critical part shows up in or around your body. How do you know this part is around? Do you hear it? Do you sense it?"

"That's an interesting question. It's kind of always there, I mean, I don't know that it's never *not* around. It just gets louder sometimes."

"Okay, and now, as you check in, how loud is it? What is it saying?"

"You know, after last night, it's pissed; it's reminding me of how I fucked up again and it says I'm just going to keep doing this. It makes me feel tight, kind of braced."

"As you notice this part, how do you feel toward it?"

Mara put her head in her hands. "I really, really hate it. It ruins everything. If I could just be free of this part . . . but that's never going to happen."

Finding Calm Amid Polarizations

The last question I'd posed to Mara—"How do you feel toward the critical part?"—is pivotal in the IFS model. It gauges the degree to which the Self is present or, conversely, occluded by parts. If she had answered my question with any of the 8 Cs (or qualities such as openness or spaciousness), it would have let me know that she had access to her core wisdom—that she was, in IFS terms, *Self-led*. If that had been the case, she would have been more likely to have a positive interaction with her critical part because it would have sensed her openness and lack of judgment. It would have been more likely to reveal itself.

However, Mara's response ("I really, really hate it; it ruins everything") indicated she was not Self-led. Instead, it let me know that she was now blended with another part—a firefighter who disliked and wanted to get rid of the critical part. Not only did the firefighter prevent her from being curious about the critical manager, it also alienated the critic, who became more closed off and unwilling to communicate.

If this pattern is familiar to you, you have experienced how out of control and chaotic polarized parts can make you feel. If you're like many people, you deal with that by making certain parts the problem and trying to get them to change. Indeed, as you get to know your protective parts, you'll likely find that you like some more than others. You may notice, for example, that you feel proud of the protectors who are assertive, disciplined, or productive and ashamed of the ones who freeze, dissociate, or use food or other substances to numb out or distract. The "you" who holds these prejudices is another protector who is responding to legacy or cultural legacy burdens that elevate some protective strategies over others. As Staci Haines (2019) observes, "social and cultural conditions tend to accept and encourage certain survival responses in certain peoples, genders, and groups, and not in others" (p. 104). It's something I often observed when I was the director of a day treatment program for eating disorders. Clients with bulimia and binge eating disorder routinely shamed themselves for not having the self-control (as they perceived it) exhibited by clients with anorexia.

A central tenet of IFS, one that will be repeated often in this book, is that there are "no bad parts" (Schwartz, 2021). Widening the lens to hold all of the members of your internal system with compassion and with the clarity that each is valuable is the first step in helping parts relax and trust you. When they're not seen as "the problem" and are instead appreciated for how they've been trying to help you, your parts can relax a bit, especially when they see that you're able to get the parts they're polarized with to ease up too.

Establishing trust with your protectors takes time and patience as you keep showing them that you're not the little kid you were when they first took on their roles—that you now have the capacity to handle things in a different way. As your protectors trust you more, they will let you know what they fear would happen if they were to give up their jobs and allow the Self to heal the vulnerable parts of your system. When this happens, you're on your way to realizing the goals of IFS:

1. Liberate parts from the roles they've been forced into so they can be who they are designed to be.

2. Restore trust in the Self and its ability to lead the system.

3. Reharmonize the inner system so parts collaborate with greater ease.

4. Become more Self-led in your interactions with other people.

In the following chapter, you'll learn how to unblend from protective parts and establish trusting relationships with them, which allows you to understand the fears they harbor about easing up on or letting go of their protective strategies.

Chapter 3

Unblending and Befriending

"We live in a world that constantly, ruthlessly judges our bodies—particularly if our bodies are anything other than white, thin, abled, free of scars and blemishes, or otherwise marked by difference. Those judgments are upheld and deepened by institutional practices and cultural beliefs that keep fat people, disabled people, people with disfigurements, and more on the margins—not because of *how we feel about our own bodies*, but because of how *other people treat our bodies*."

–Aubrey Gordon

Natalie was a sixty-three-year-old guidance counselor at a high school for the performing arts in a large city. Married with two grown children, she first came to see me a few years ago for help in dealing with an "inner critic." She described herself as relatively happy in most areas of her life—she liked her job and enjoyed her relationships with her husband and two adult children.

But as she prepared for her daughter's wedding, she was consumed with intense anxiety about her appearance. All she could think about was how she would look, especially in comparison to her daughter's fiancé's mother, whom she regarded as much more attractive. "She always looks good in whatever she wears. I am going to look awful standing next to her."

As she tried on dresses, Natalie heard a voice that was so mean that it startled her. "What the fuck is wrong with you? You knew this was coming, and you did nothing about it!"

She felt a rush of adrenaline as a diet-minded part considered the time remaining before the wedding. How much weight could she lose if she worked really hard?

This internal calculation was familiar. In a vague but persistent way, it reflected how the diet-minded part of Natalie marked time— planning for and failing to lose weight by the summer, by Thanksgiving, after the New Year, by her birthday, and so on. Most of the time, this part remained in the periphery, so although Natalie noticed it, she was able to brush it aside. Now, however, it responded to the ruthlessness of the critical voice by anxiously searching for the diet that would result in the most weight loss before the wedding. The pain she felt about this, juxtaposed with the joy she wanted to feel about the wedding, motivated her to get help.

As Natalie described to me what was going on, she became more upset. I understood why she was feeling overwhelmed. Natalie had several competing parts with strong feelings and agendas they all wanted her to acknowledge or meet.

The first thing I needed to do was help Natalie identify and separate from the parts who were making themselves known in different ways, so I reflected back what I heard. "I'm hearing that things are generally good. Your relationships and work are satisfying, and most of the time, you feel good about yourself. That said, there's a part of you who's always worried about your weight in a low-key, chronic way that has recently gotten that much more intense with your daughter's wedding coming up. And that critical voice is making other parts feel anxious. Am I getting that right?"

"Yes," Natalie replied. "That's right. Ever since my daughter got engaged, I have been so stressed out about what I'm going to look like and what I'm going to wear. I don't want to feel like this! I want it to be a happy time."

"Of course. It makes sense that you would be really upset about this, that you want this to be a time to celebrate."

Natalie responded, "Yes, but all I can think about is how I'm going to look."

I could hear that this critical part was definitely not welcomed by at least one other part, so I knew that I needed to help Natalie to get the parts who disliked the critic to relax back a bit so she could get to know the critical part better.

I said, "Natalie, see if the parts who are upset with the critical part would be willing to give you space so you can listen to it. Once we know why it's so critical, we can help it and the parts it's protecting."

"I'm not sure. Hearing the criticism makes me feel bad. And, honestly, it feels shallow to be concerned about this."

Differentiating Parts to Access Self

As you learned in the last chapter, when parts blend, they merge their thoughts, feelings, sensations, images, and memories with the Self. Blending with parts is natural and, in itself, is not a problem. When parts blend, they can provide the Self with vital information. A good example is an angry part who blends with the Self to convey the need for better boundaries. Sometimes parts need to fully blend for a bit so they can feel that your Self really understands them. However, when parts are burdened and resist unblending, as Natalie's parts were doing, they block your access to the Self. This makes it impossible for the Self to be a healing resource for your parts.

As a point of comparison, it may help you to recall times when you've been with a child who is extremely upset and is charged up or shut down. In their activated state, it's hard to help them because they either can't take anything in or you can't make out what they need from you. In these moments, it's helpful to remain calm and to let them know that you're with them, gently reminding them that if they slow down a little and speak about what's making them so upset, you'll be much more likely to be able to help them.

This is what Natalie's parts needed and could not yet get from her Self, so I shared my own Self-energy with her by exuding some of the 8 Cs (qualities of Self). I extended my own *compassion* and *clarity* to engage Natalie's. In a *calm* voice, I shared that I was *confident* that each of her parts had its reasons for feeling or behaving the way it did; if she could take some time to get *curious* about them, they would let us know more about themselves.

With this reminder, Natalie relaxed a bit. She felt calmer and more open to getting to know the different parts that dress shopping had incited. I suggested she take a few minutes to jot down or draw the different parts she noticed coming up. Externalizing parts in this way can facilitate separating or *unblending* from them. This can be especially helpful when you notice a number of parts coming up at the same time or if you find that focusing your attention inside feels too overwhelming, which is often the case if you've experienced a lot of trauma, body-related or otherwise.

In Natalie's case, several parts had such strong negative feelings that she found it difficult to distinguish one from the other until she made note of them on paper. Once she could see them in front of her, she got a clearer sense of them and how they related to each other. For example, Natalie noticed an anxious part who worried about how she'd measure up to the groom's mother, an appearance-focused part who felt critical of her body, a diet-minded part who searched for a way to lose weight fast, and a protector she called her "superior" part because of its holier-than-thou attitude toward the other parts and their "superficial" concerns.

When I asked Natalie which part needed her attention the most, she immediately identified the part who was critical of her appearance.

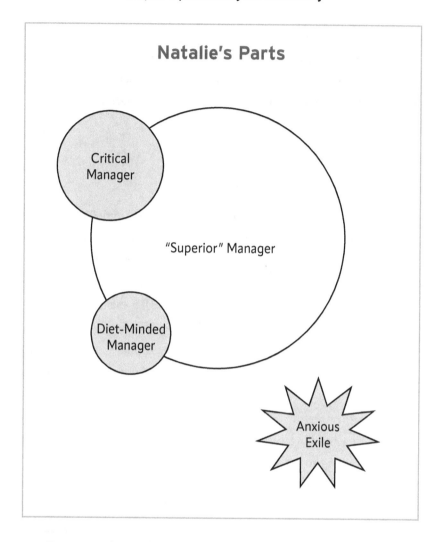

Decisions about where to start often follow from this kind of needs assessment. The protector who is the most distressed—or distressing to the other parts of the system—is typically the one you focus on first. This is known as the *target part*. Before you proceed, however, it's important to see if there are any other parts who object. If there are, then the target part will sense that and not open up.

It might be helpful to think about it like this: When you're really upset about something and you want to talk about it with someone, what do you need from them? Chances are that you first need that other person to give you room to share what's upsetting you. Then you need them to validate your feelings without passing judgment or making suggestions. You also don't want them to tell you that your feelings are wrong, silly, or superficial. This is exactly what parts need too.

Facilitating Self-to-Part Relationships: The 6 Fs

In her role as a guidance counselor, Natalie was accustomed to checking in with herself and helping her students do the same. However, she tended to be led by pragmatic managers who preferred problem-solving to feeling. She also had parts who would handle her upset by minimizing it and urging her to be grateful for what she had.

Like Natalie, you may be used to thinking about or analyzing your experience. Often, thinking and analyzing parts have theories about why other parts do what they do. While they may be onto something some of the time, they're often only partially correct, and sometimes, they're considerably off the mark. That's because the information that comes from a thinking part reflects the bias of that part instead of the part you're trying to get to know. In addition, since thinking parts are cerebral, they don't pick up on a great deal of information—namely, the feelings and sensations of parts that are held in the body. In addition to aligning with the dominant culture's reverence of the intellect, the protectors know that the exiles' experiences are "stored in the tissues, and they don't want to be crushed again by overwhelming sensations" (McConnell, 2020, p. 80).

With IFS, you shift from *thinking about* or analyzing your parts to *relating to* them, using a series of steps designed to identify and more or less interview the part, much like you might with someone you were just meeting. These steps are known as the 6 Fs (Focus, Find, Feel toward, Flesh out, beFriend, and Fears), and they facilitate unblending from a target part so you can begin to establish a trusting relationship between it and the Self.

Many people find they can effectively employ these steps on their own once they've had some experience with IFS and if their system is not extremely burdened or activated. If you have many parts who carry burdens related to food, your body, or any number of things, you will find it helpful to meet with an IFS therapist who can help you identify and unblend from your parts. In addition to helping you get to know the different parts of your system, an IFS therapist can lend their own Self-energy to the parts of you who can't imagine allowing, or won't allow, your system to change.

In the next section, you'll learn how Natalie used the 6 Fs to get to know one of her protectors, what led it to take on its job, and what it hoped to accomplish. As Natalie's experience illustrates, these steps allowed her to appreciate the protector's motivations and get its permission to access the exiled parts it had tried to ward off.

Don't get overly concerned with the order of these steps—IFS practitioners differ in their preferences about this—and don't get too attached to them (e.g., feeling like you must methodically go through each one). Instead, consider them guideposts to getting to know the inhabitants of your inner world.

Focus

IFS starts when you identify a problem and notice the thoughts, images, emotions, and sensations that relate to that problem. Selecting the one you most want to work with or change, you *focus* your attention on it to see how you experience it. If you're used to meditating or engaging in mindfulness practices, you may be used to observing your thoughts and feelings from a place of acceptance. This is an important first step in the IFS model, as parts make themselves known in various ways. You may hear their voices, as Natalie did when she blended with the critical part who lambasted her for not losing weight, or you may sense or feel them. Numbness, dizziness, pain, tightness, and fluctuations in breathing, heart rate, and temperature are several of the many ways parts make themselves known somatically. Parts may also show up in persistent thoughts, feelings, or images. All of these are what IFS calls *trailheads* because they are emanations from parts that will lead you to the target part if you stay focused on them.

Paying close attention to the various thoughts, feelings, images, and sensations, no matter how subtle, is key to being able to notice parts and get familiar with their customary ways of expressing themselves. That song that won't stop playing in the back of your mind? The image that just flashed by? They might just be a message from a part who wants you to know something about its experience or what it needs from you.

Sometimes you may have an immediate sense of the protector—what it looks or sounds like or how old or young it is. With some parts, however, it can take a little time and attention to observe how it shows up in your thoughts or in the body.

Find

This step involves paying close attention to how the part manifests and *finding* where it shows up in or around your body. The part of Natalie who felt critical of her appearance spoke in a tone that sounded just like her father's. It showed up in her furrowed brow. In turn, it fueled an angry and exasperated voice that told her she was shallow for caring so much about her appearance. As Natalie focused on that voice, she noticed how it connected to a bracing sensation on the right side of her chest. "It's like a tight clenching, especially over here," she said, as she placed her left hand on her right clavicle.

Protectors are typically forced into their protective roles when you are quite young. The strategies they adopt to cope are those that make sense or are available at the time. In challenging or dangerous environments, young children often have extremely limited ways to express distress or self-soothe; some of these can include mental processes such as fantasizing, ruminating, or dissociating. Other ways are more somatic and can include eating/not eating, sleeping/not sleeping, pulling hair or skin, nail biting, and various kinds of somatic ailments (e.g., headaches, stomachaches and other gastrointestinal disturbances, rashes). You may have parts who learned to communicate via somatic symptoms in ways that members of your family did. You also carry in your body the genetic imprint of intergenerational traumas from your family or culture. Attending to subtle and more obvious feelings and sensations will help you get to know much more about your internal system.

Feel Toward

Once Natalie identified the critical part as the target part and observed how it manifested in a tight furrowing of her brow, I asked her how she *felt toward* the part. As you learned earlier, this is a key question in the IFS model because it reveals whether you are blended with other parts. You know you're blended with another part if you feel anything other than the 8 Cs—qualities of Self—toward the target part (e.g., "I hate it," "It's hopeless," "It's not a part, it's me"). You may also notice that you reflexively say, "Sure, I'm curious or open"—but when you take a moment to check in, you find that this response is coming from another part who isn't truly interested. If it seems too easy, it probably is, so it's a good idea to double-check. A good way to do so is to ask yourself if your heart is open to the part.

Remember that protectors tend to be stuck in the past, employing strategies that are no longer effective and that come with costly downsides. They do so because they're convinced their strategies are essential to keeping the system safe and, *at one time or in some way,* it's likely that they were. Some of their protective activity may still be necessary, depending on the environment. Your protectors think you're still a child and they don't know or trust your Self to handle things. They are wary of any attempts, internal or external, to get them to change. That's why when you're trying to get to know a target part, other protective parts who want to eliminate the target part, or make sure you don't mess with it, may interfere with your attempt to get to know it.

"Feeling toward" a part is a gauge of how much of your Self-energy (compassion, calm, courage, etc.) is available to be in relationship with your target part.

Natalie's experience serves as a good example. In our initial meeting, she described a polarization between the appearance-focused protector who was critical of her weight and the "superior" protector who hated it for being so shallow. While, at first, she was able to get the "superior" part to separate and relax back, this unblending was short-lived. Several minutes later, as she checked to see how she felt toward the appearance-focused part, the "superior" part immediately jumped back in.

"I really don't like this part; it's not who I want to be. It's so superficial."

Since the "superior" part didn't respond to Natalie's efforts to unblend, she had to shift her attention to it and make it the target part instead. While she was then able to focus on the "superior" one without the critic interfering in turn, this is not often what happens. You'll discover that it may be necessary to do some negotiating with the protector you're *not* engaging with before it will give you room to relate to the target part. It usually needs some assurance that you won't let the target part dominate. When that doesn't work, because there's so much distrust between protectors, you may have to meet with both parts, much like a therapist or mediator, to help both sides trust the Self to keep each protector's interests in mind. As with any conflict, internal and external, both parties' concerns must be respected and attended to, including following up to make sure all involved feel understood.

In this case, Natalie was able to get permission from her critical part to shift to the "superior" part. She focused inside and located the "superior" part, once again noticing its clenching on the right side of her body under her clavicle. I asked how she felt toward it.

"I understand why this part feels this way. A lot of me thinks it's superficial to be so focused on what I'm going to look like. I mean, I'm not the bride."

With this, I detected other parts who didn't have concerns about the "superior" part but who agreed with it! It can be tricky to be what IFS calls a good *parts detector* when it comes to these parts who cheerlead the part you're trying to get to know. While they don't seem problematic, their enthusiasm about the target part will make it harder for you to get a true sense of the target part.

"See if the parts who agree with this protector would give us some room to get to know it better. Are they willing?"

Natalie said, "Let me check. Yes, they're willing. I guess I am a little interested in knowing why this part is as upset as it is."

While Natalie wasn't wildly enthusiastic, her response indicated that she had some *curiosity*, meaning she had some access to the Self-energy she would need to engage and get to know the target part. However, given the tepid response of being "a little" interested, I would need to keep checking in with Natalie, assessing how she felt toward the part as she learned more about it. I had to be sure she wasn't blending with other parts—both those who allied themselves with the target part and wanted it to stay as well as those who disliked it.

Flesh Out

Now that Natalie felt some curiosity about her "superior" protector, she was ready to learn more about it. *Fleshing out* is a rapport-building step that helps you get a better sense of the part. This process is analogous to what happens when you're interested in getting to know someone: You ask them to share more about themselves so you can move beyond your initial impression. Among other things, when you flesh out a part, you may learn how old it is, the role it was forced to take on in the system, and its gender, temperament, intentions, and perspective.

As Natalie focused on the "superior" part who told her she was shallow for fixating on her appearance, she noted that she couldn't see it but could sense its indignation.

"Okay, how close are you to that part?"

"It feels pretty close. I can feel it right here," she said, pointing to the right side of her chest. It's tense."

"Fleshing out" involves becoming more familiar with the protector. Our parts can present themselves in different ways—as images, thoughts, sensations, or feelings.

"Let it know you're interested in learning more about it. See how it reacts."

"It's irritated. Turned to the side. I can't really see it, but it's like an angry kid, with her arms crossed—not really wanting anything to do with me."

Noticing that Natalie had referred to her part as both "it" and then "her," I followed her lead. I know how important it is to avoid making assumptions about parts, their gender or otherwise, and to ask if I am unclear.

"Okay, how are you being with this part? Are you still open to getting to know her?"

"I'm still open."

"Let her know that. See what she wants you to know about herself, like how old she is, and what she's trying to do for you."

"She says she's many different ages, but I get the sense that she's not super young, more like thirteen or fourteen, something like that."

I stayed quiet as Natalie kept her attention on the part.

"She says she's angry that I'm being like this, that I'm so stressed about this, about how I'm going to look."

"See if she can tell you why she's angry. What does it mean to her that other parts of you are worried about that?"

Natalie closed her eyes to focus on the part and said, "I don't know. All I'm getting is a *This is not who I am.*"

"Do you know what she means? See if there's more she wants to say about that."

Natalie took a deep breath and sighed. "I don't want to be someone who is consumed with all this worry about being fat, about getting older, all of that."

Hearing the voice of the "superior" part, I asked, "Is that what the 'superior' part is saying? Is that her role, to get you to not be concerned about all of that?"

Natalie nodded.

"How long has she been doing that?" I asked.

Natalie shrugged. "I don't know. Since I was a teenager, thirteen or fourteen."

"Ask her if she can show you or tell you her earliest memory of trying to get you to not be concerned about what you look like."

"There's not a single memory that comes to mind. I just remember feeling so mad at my parents, especially my father, for being so focused on my body. They were always so worried about me, about how I dressed, how big I was. My whole family is like that, always talking about food and how much weight they need to lose."

"So this part is mad about that?"

Natalie paused for a moment. "Yes, this part has zero tolerance for any of that. It refuses to obsess about these things. Which is why it's so upset about this."

I replied, "You mean, it's upset that another part of you is so focused on and critical of your appearance?"

Natalie nodded. "Yes, it hates that part."

Natalie had identified an important polarization in her internal system: one manager who was committed to not thinking about her body very much and another manager who "obsessed" with how she could improve her appearance. Natalie referred to the part who hated the critical part as a "superior" part since it judged the part she called "the critic." While this shorthand was easier for Natalie, it's important to remember that each of these parts had a range of thoughts and feelings other than the ones with which they came to be identified.

BeFriend

For many parts, a certain amount of trust needs to be built in order for them to believe that things could actually be different in the system. *BeFriending* is the step that focuses on this trust building. As you would if you were reconnecting with someone from whom you've been estranged for some time, you get curious about what this part has been trying to do for you. You let the part know *you* care about what it's been like for the part to be in its role and how it feels toward you (the Self) now that you are back in connection.

Befriending happens fairly quickly for some protective parts. They feel open to meeting the Self, and even if they have some concerns about shifting out of their constraining roles, they feel excited or hopeful about the possibility of being able to be relieved of their responsibilities. For other protectors, however, befriending is more complicated and will take longer, requiring more reassurance from you that their strategies made (and may still make) sense, that you aren't trying to force them to change, and that your Self can handle their concerns. Speaking about her experience in meeting with BIPOC clients and clinicians, Tamala Floyd (2023) notes that an extended befriending process is often necessary because of the protectors' lack of trust in the Self and a dependence on the protectors "who have had to manage historical threats" (p. 90).

As Natalie learned more about her "superior" part, I asked her to see how she was feeling toward this target part. I wanted to make sure she still had access to her Self-energy, and her response confirmed that she did.

"I feel a little calmer. It helps me to be reminded that this is just a part of me and that it's trying to help—because it can make me feel really bad sometimes. I don't like thinking of myself as shallow. But I kind of respect this part when I consider how strong she is and has had to be."

"Great. Natalie, can she feel your respect? What is it like for her?"

"It feels good. She feels like I'm understanding her better."

"Wonderful. Let her know you're interested in learning more. First, ask her how old she thinks you are."

"She thinks I'm five."

"Okay, let her know how old you actually are and see how she responds to that."

Natalie grimaced as she related what she heard from the part. "She's like 'Are you kidding?' She can't believe I'm that old. She thinks I should be doing better, that I should be above all this."

"She's angry with you? How do you respond to her?"

"I'm letting her know I understand why she would feel that way."

"Can she take in what you're saying?"

"Yes, she's more open, less tight. Her arms are at her sides now and she's turned a little more toward me. But she's tough. She isn't going to let down her guard easily."

"Okay, and what do you want her to know about that?"

"It makes sense. She doesn't know me. I think I've thought she *was* me. She's a big part of how I see myself."

"Great. Let her know that you understand why she doesn't trust you very much right now. Is she willing to let you to get a little closer to her?"

"A little. She's okay with me sitting across from her, like five or six feet away."

"Okay, great. See how she feels when you are that close."

"She says she doesn't want me to get any closer. It's a visceral *no!* I let her know I respect that."

As Natalie extended her curiosity and compassion to her protector, the part gradually opened up and connected to her. Still, she was wary of Natalie and didn't want her to get too close. This mistrust makes sense. Like most protectors, this part of Natalie was forced into her role when Natalie was quite young. She hadn't known Natalie's Self to be a resource on which she could rely. Natalie would need to spend more time with this part to earn her trust.

Over the course of several sessions, Natalie kept coming back to focus on this part of herself. While not technically a "C" quality, Natalie's *consistency* about checking in with this part in between sessions was instrumental in helping it soften a bit. Each time Natalie related to this "superior" part from her Self instead of from another protector, the part developed increasingly more trust that Natalie didn't have an agenda to defend, get rid of, or criticize her. As a result, the "superior" part became willing to share more about herself and her role in the system.

"She's fierce. She says she refuses to get caught up thinking about what I should look like. It's all the stuff my parents were so obsessed with. They couldn't understand why I couldn't be more feminine, why I couldn't lose weight. It bothered them that I didn't care about any of it."

Natalie continued to relate more about this part of herself. "Other parts of me would get caught up in caring about all of that, but this part kept me focused on what was right for me."

I asked Natalie, "As she's reminding you of this, how are you feeling toward her?"

She replied, "I appreciate how hard she's worked to forge her own path when she really didn't have any support to do that."

"Let her know you value her and see how she responds."

Natalie looked bemused. "This part is proud. She likes that she helped me stay true to myself and not let a part take over who pretended to be who they wanted me to be. This is the part who goes to bat for my students so they can be who they are."

I asked Natalie, "This 'superior' part—is there more she'd like you to know about her and what she's been trying to do for you?"

"I'm not sure what this means, but I just got an image of myself at that age, when I was fourteen. I came home and heard my parents fighting. My mother was crying—it was hard to make out the words—and my dad was yelling, saying mean things about her. She came out of the room and looked beaten down. I was so angry with my father, but when I tried to defend her, she got angry at me and defended him. She blamed herself for getting him angry. This 'superior' part is telling me that she never wanted me to be in that position, dependent on a man and vulnerable to his insults."

"Ask her if there's more she wants you to know about what that was like for her."

"It was lonely. My father didn't like me very much. He blamed me for being difficult, for not being more like my mother and sister."

"What does she mean by that, about being more like your mom and sister?"

"They didn't challenge or confront him when he said crazy shit. Like when he told me, in front of everyone, that my butt and legs were getting too big. Or when he commented, which he always did, about how much I ate and how I needed to watch it."

"What does this part want you to know about that?"

"It was humiliating—enraging—to have him be so focused on my body. That's why this 'superior' part dislikes the part who criticizes me for what I look like. It's revolting to her."

"Do you understand why she feels that way?"

Natalie nodded.

I continued, saying, "Let her know you understand why she feels this way, and also ask her if she likes her job of being tough. See what she has to say."

Natalie was quiet for a moment. "She shrugged when I asked her that. She says she likes it fine. It is what it is."

This exchange between Natalie and her "superior" part illustrates how effective befriending is at establishing enough trust between a part and the

Self that the part becomes willing to talk about its role in the system and how it feels about it. Befriending sets the stage for the final F: *fears*.

Fears

The last step in working with a protective part is to find out what it *fears* would happen if it shifted out of its protective role and allowed the Self to take over. Parts take on their jobs for one of three reasons: They've been hurt in the past, they're protecting a part who's been hurt *or is being* hurt, or they're countering other protectors whose strategies conflict with theirs. Before they'll agree to shift out of these extreme roles, protectors need to know that you'll address the fears they hold about making this change. You'll learn more about negotiating with parts to address their fears and help them unblend more in the next chapter.

By asking the protector what it fears would happen if it didn't do its job, you learn either about exiles it protects or other protectors it's polarized with. When the protectors are reassured that the Self can address their concerns, they give their permission to go to those parts.

When Natalie was ready to approach this final step, she asked the "superior" part what it feared would happen if it stopped doing its job. It responded in a pragmatic manner, which was consistent with this part's no-nonsense attitude.

"The 'superior' part says she's the sole reason why I don't get sucked into my family's mindset of hating and trying to change my body."

The more Natalie got to know her "superior" part, the more she appreciated the part's strength and dedication. Natalie saw what a brave young girl she'd been, bucking the system around her so she could retain her identity in a patriarchal family that rewarded loyalty and conformity.

However, as Natalie continued to explore the "superior" part's feelings about her role in the system, the part admitted how tiresome it was to keep fending off the critic so Natalie's exiles wouldn't get hurt by its criticism.

"It's tedious to have to keep pushing aside this nagging feeling that I should be doing something to look better. And then something like this wedding comes up and it's all the critical part can think about."

As tired as it was of warding off the critical part, the "superior" protector didn't yet trust that it was safe to ease up on its stance toward the critic. She needed Natalie's Self to know more about her concerns and to address them before she would be willing to take this risk. As you'll see in the next chapter, Natalie continued to befriend her "superior" protector and learned that this part had good reason to fear the part who, like her father, could be so harsh.

Blend, Unblend, Repeat

It's natural for parts to blend, for this is a primary way they share information with the Self. When parts are burdened, however, they become extreme in how they do this. Exiles blend because they are desperate to be witnessed for what they've endured, while protectors quickly overtake the system to enact their protective strategies.

You may notice how the part of you who is really furious may calm down for a moment before getting enraged again. Or the part who's scared that you can't handle a suicidal part will keep interrupting with its fears about what will happen if you go there. It's important to keep in mind that protectors have their reasons for doing what they do. They will keep blending until they feel that you, from a place of Self-energy, care about and can act to either address the protectors they polarize with or unburden the exiles they protect, who are stuck in the past with their pain.

When you remind parts that you can't help them if you *are* them (i.e., totally blended with their thoughts, feelings, and sensations), it can help them relax back so the Self can *be with* them and listen to their concerns. It helps protectors to understand that unblending is an ongoing process, not a single event, especially when there are many exiles who are burdened in the system. It is also helpful for them to learn that exiles are not inherently liabilities but, rather, important members of the system whose valuable qualities become available when the protectors open space so the exiles can be healed by the Self. It takes time to establish new relationships with your protectors, and repeatedly recognizing, blending with, and unblending from protectors is central to developing trusting Self-to-part relationships.

With or without the help of a therapist, you'll notice as you practice the 6 Fs that it usually gets easier to unblend from parts on your own. There are a couple of reasons for this. First, the act of focusing inside to discern the different parts organically allows for some separation and access to your Self. Second, the more you focus your attention inside, the easier it will be to detect various parts because you become more familiar with how they show up in the body, in your thoughts, and in your behaviors. Last, as you help parts relax and show them that you care about and will address their fears, they become more willing to separate. The following illustration depicts the 6 Fs and provides some information to assist you in determining when to get some extra support.

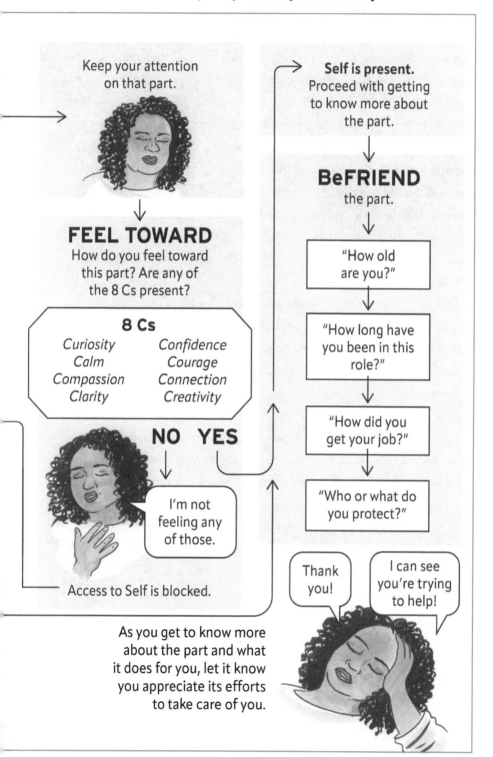

Keep your attention on that part.

Self is present.
Proceed with getting to know more about the part.

BeFRIEND
the part.

FEEL TOWARD
How do you feel toward this part? Are any of the 8 Cs present?

8 Cs
Curiosity   Confidence
Calm   Courage
Compassion   Connection
Clarity   Creativity

NO   YES

I'm not feeling any of those.

Access to Self is blocked.

"How old are you?"

"How long have you been in this role?"

"How did you get your job?"

"Who or what do you protect?"

Thank you!

I can see you're trying to help!

As you get to know more about the part and what it does for you, let it know you appreciate its efforts to take care of you.

Something to keep in mind is that some of the cultural burdens that disconnect you from your core wisdom (e.g., White supremacist values of perfectionism, urgency, either/or thinking) can impact how you approach the IFS model. When you blend with the parts who hold these cultural burdens, you may notice a sense of urgency about unblending from protectors to "get into Self," placing particular importance on being "calm" and quickly moving past protectors to heal your exiles. You may view Self-energy as "good" and parts as "bad," and you may become critical when your "progress" is neither swift nor linear, as happens when there are many burdened exiles and protectors who harbor fears about change, especially when the environment continues to activate your parts.

It's helpful to get to know the protectors who are saddled with these beliefs. Let them know that they, like all parts, are inherently valuable and that you appreciate how they've been trying to keep you safe. Remind them that while healing the exiles is ultimately what provides the greatest transformation to the internal system (because it liberates not only them but the protectors), the initial steps of unblending from and befriending protectors can be life changing. It's also helpful to remind these parts that when healing is slow and circular, as when you find yourself eating in ways you don't like or feeling pulled to diet again, it is simply a trailhead signaling the need for further intervention from the Self.

If you are trying to get curious about your internal system on your own, you may find it helpful to externalize the parts of your system by mapping them out, as Natalie did, or by using various props to represent them. Rocks, shells, sticks, scarves, stuffed animals, and other objects can all be used to represent parts. Other people use whiteboards, sketch pads, sand trays, clay, or different forms of movement to differentiate their parts. You may also want to try interviewing your parts, like you would if you were getting to know someone. Questions you might ask include how old the protector is, how and when it got its job, whether it likes what it does, and its concerns about taking a break from or completely shifting out of its role.

As with most everything, you will notice that different parts will respond to certain techniques and not to others. Some parts, for example, won't have words but will communicate through images or sensations. Other parts will convey their experience through thoughts and analysis. Parts who don't trust the Self will initially be less forthcoming but share more as you follow up with them. The bottom line is that your parts will start to trust you when you keep coming back to learn more about them, so use whatever strategies support consistent connection.

Chapter 4

Negotiating and Getting Permission

"Sitting with her I choose not to leave
And the hole in her chest heals
I hold her close
Her warm tears melt my walls
She looks up and sees there is no roof to her jail
She can finally soar away"

–Jessica Semaan

As you've learned in the first three chapters, it's both helpful and necessary to recognize when a part is "doing the talking." Once you realize this, you have the opportunity to be the one who listens to the part that's been blending with you.

The trouble is that there's often more than one part around, especially if you're distressed. In Natalie's case, there were at least four parts who showed up around the wedding dress issue: one who was very anxious about how she would look compared to the groom's mother, one who was very critical of her when she thought about dress shopping, one who was planning to diet, and one who felt shallow about even talking about any of it.

Since parts are like people who want and need to be listened to with openness and understanding, you need a way to be with them one at a time so they can get that from you. This underscores the importance of being a keen parts detector who can identify and listen to each part with genuine curiosity and intervene when another part tries to take over. If other parts with different views—or parts who harbor concerns about the target part—are lingering nearby, the target will in *no way* feel safe to tell you about itself. Therefore, you need to get the other parts to relax and give a little room so you can listen to the one who needs your attention the most.

Many parts initially resist unblending, even for just a little while. Remember that many protectors are typically young and were forced to take on their roles by stressful or traumatic situations. They may have learned that hating your body helped you fit in or receive less criticism from others. That sneaking food or skipping meals helped you feel better when things got tough. That people-pleasing was the best way to avoid being abandoned or hurt. These strategies made sense *at the time and in the context in which they developed*. Even if they aren't necessary or even helpful now, your protectors will persist in taking care of you in the way they learned how. They need you to update them on your current situation and help them trust that it's safe for them to consider trying something new because you, from Self, can heal the parts they have been working so hard to protect or banish.

In some cases, a protector's "unwillingness" to unblend is a reasonable response to current external conditions that call for the protector's continued deployment. This is particularly true for members of groups that have been historically marginalized by the dominant culture. As Natalie Gutiérrez (2022) notes, "The survival tools that keep you safe in a dangerous relationship or environment can feel too risky to release while you're still there" (p. 94). In these cases, it's important to validate the protector's prior experiences of harmful treatment and discernment of ongoing threat. When the protective part feels seen and heard, it will be more likely to briefly go off-duty for a time and in a context that feels safe to it (e.g., with a trusted friend, colleague, therapist, or affinity group) so that the Self can help the wounded exiles release some of their burdens. With less vulnerability to guard against internally, and with more access to your Self-energy, the protector may not have to work as hard, nor feel so alone, even in the face of ongoing stress or harm from the external environment. In other words, while this won't put an end to any external harm that may come your way, it will transform what happens in your internal system in terms of how you react to the harm and how you choose to take care of yourself in the wake of it.

The problem is that your parts are like kids who have been left alone, completely or for long periods of time, without a competent parent. They often don't trust that there is a Self who can take care of them. Therefore, when you extend Self-energy to a part, it can have any number of reactions, including relief at finally being seen, anger at having been neglected for so long, and, often, skepticism or hopelessness regarding the Self's capacity to take care of the system.

This is particularly true for protectors who focus on food and the body as a way to contain pain and prevent more harm as you move through the world. They typically have years or decades of experience doing what they do. Some of them don't recall ever having felt anything even resembling the grounding presence and inner spaciousness of the Self. All they know is that they've had to keep fighting with other parts whose ideas about how to keep you safe conflict with their own. The part who says, "You've had enough to eat" watches as other parts who feel deprived or need distraction reach for more food. In the same way, these deprived parts, who long to eat food they truly enjoy, watch as the critical or dieting parts take over with a new set of dreary rules.

Not only have your protectors not known your Self to be a comforting presence, but they also haven't experienced much Self-energy elsewhere. They are constantly provoked by other people's parts—online, in the news, and in casual conversations with family, friends, and colleagues who feel compelled to talk about their own internal battles (e.g., "I can't believe I ate all of that" or "I look disgusting") or who judge you or other people, often in ways they believe are well-intended (e.g., "Don't you think you'd feel better if you just ____?"). With so little incentive to give up their habitual ways of thinking and feeling, it makes good sense that parts need a lot of help from you before they become willing to risk shifting out of their customary roles.

In the last chapter, you learned about the 6 Fs, a guide for identifying and separating from protective parts so you can relate to them from your Self. This chapter will elaborate on the last F—*fears*—by revisiting Mara's and Natalie's journeys (and by introducing Christina) and illustrating how to negotiate with the protectors so they feel understood for their fears and more trusting of the Self.

Generally speaking, these negotiations between the Self and the protectors involve conveying hope to the protectors that if they risk something new (i.e., handing the reins over to the Self), the parts they protect can be healed. Once this happens, they will be freed from their constraining roles. For example, if you have parts who avoid exercise (because striving managers have often pushed the body beyond what is comfortable or safe), you might offer, "I know it might not seem so, but the part who 'overdoes' it is also trying to help in its own way. If you knew that I could help that part so it didn't override what feels good or enough, would you be willing to ease up on how often you shut down my motivation for physical activity?" In turn, the manager who "overdoes" it might need to hear you say, "I know there are times when the part who avoids exercise altogether has taken over, sometimes for months. If you relaxed a bit, I could get to know that part and help it so it didn't need to shut things down to that degree." Negotiating with protectors often involves reassuring them that you as Self are not young and vulnerable and that you can handle them as well as the exiles and the intense feelings, sensations, and memories they hold. As you'll see, when protectors feel that your Self understands their fears and will act to address them in relationship with the other parts of the system, they will agree to open space.

"Nothing Works"

Mara had been working with me to get to know the protectors who kept her locked in a painful cycle of restricting and "overeating." She was beginning to consider how each of these parts had been trying to take care of her, and she even noticed having a little more compassion for herself. However, one night she found herself eating in a way that made parts of her feel extremely out of control.

"It's like this every time I go out to dinner with these friends. I started out with good intentions, but then not only did I eat the bread, I drank too much and ended up getting dessert. And not just sharing dessert but eating my *own* dessert. And because once I get started, I can't stop, it just continued from there when I got home."

When she came to session the next day, she was blended with a part who was quite hopeless and distressed. "I've tried everything. I've worked with dietitians, I've tried mindful eating and Intuitive Eating, I'm trying to do what you're talking about, and *nothing* works. At the end of the day, I just can't control myself."

I shared with Mara what I understood about her evening and its aftermath. "Tell me if this feels right to you. The part who's speaking feels hopeless. It's describing a cycle you've experienced a lot when you go out to dinner with friends. You came to dinner already blended with another part who had some ideas about what you should eat—either the bread *or* the wine. So when you had both, it activated a critical part who shamed you."

Mara nodded.

I continued, saying, "This shame made parts of you feel bad, which led another part to not only join in with dessert but to order your own, which made the critical part even more shaming. Does that sound right?"

Mara looked glum. "Yes. At that point, it was like a switch flipped. I was already thinking about what I'd eat once I got home."

I asked Mara if she could ask the hopeless part if it would be willing to give her some space so we could get to know it better. She shrugged and said, "Okay, I mean, I'm not sure what there is to find out. How should I feel after eating like that all night? I feel horrible."

I paused to see if Mara would be willing to continue.

"Alright, give me a minute," she sighed. Mara then focused her attention inside for a few moments before opening her eyes. "I'm the *tiniest* bit open to it."

Sensing that this was the best we could expect at this moment, I replied, "Great. Do you understand why this part of you feels the way it does?"

"Yes, I get why it's so discouraged. I feel sad for it."

"Okay, let it know you feel that and see how it responds."

"It says it doesn't see how this pattern is going to change, that I'm never going to be free of this—this constant flipping between trying to do better and then not."

"What is it afraid would happen if it eased up on its hopelessness?"

"It says that when I get hopeless like this, I just stop caring. I stop thinking about any of this. I just zone out and do whatever—eat, go online, or binge-watch some reality TV."

"The hopeless part protects you by shutting down and getting you to stop caring? What is it afraid would happen if it let you have some hope?"

"It says the only time I feel hopeful is when I've found some new plan, like Intuitive Eating or 'The Whole30.' The Whole30 was the latest, and that really backfired. I ended up gaining weight because I was eating too much of the foods on the 'approved' list and also combining them in ways I wasn't supposed to. Dieting, not dieting, nothing works."

"What's the worst thing about these experiences for this part?"

"Aside from the obvious—gaining weight—I get this sense of *what's wrong with me that I can't do this?* I feel so out of control."

"The hopeless part is trying to guard against another part of you who attacks you when the new plan doesn't work, is that right?"

"Yes, it's very harsh. It makes me feel like such a failure."

"The hopeless part tries to wall off the critical part who makes other parts of you feel terrible?"

"Yes. It doesn't want me to have to deal with any of this. It just wants a break from the constant criticism."

By this point, Mara had a solid connection with the hopeless part and was *fleshing out* its role in her system. She felt the hopelessness easing up as she listened to it describe how it worked to take care of her.

Mara related feeling surprised. "I've never thought of the hopelessness as a part, and definitely not as a part who is trying to take care of me," she said. "I attributed the foggy-brained, listless feeling to a kind of hangover from eating so much and feeling depressed."

Continuing to befriend her hopeless protector, Mara asked how it felt about its job.

"It says it doesn't like feeling so apathetic, but it's better than feeling agitated and having so many bad feelings."

The hopeless part let her know how exhausted it was by always having to fight with both the critical and the dieting parts.

Mara continued, saying, "It's always the way it goes. On a day like today, I start out too depressed and disgusted with myself to eat anything. I get busy with all the things I have to do. But then I start getting hungry and I'll tell myself I'm just going to eat a little, just enough so I'm not starving. But it won't feel like enough, so I'll just end up eating whatever, numbing out, and watching TV. By tomorrow, I'll wake up feeling bloated and gross—I guess that's the critical part saying that—and the dieting part will be desperate to lose weight. It'll get me to start looking for something that will bring some quick relief, like a fast or something, which won't work, and this will just keep happening."

Mara's ability to track these different parts indicated that her Self-energy was beginning to emerge. The following figure illustrates the sequence of interactions in which Mara's hopeless protector played a part.

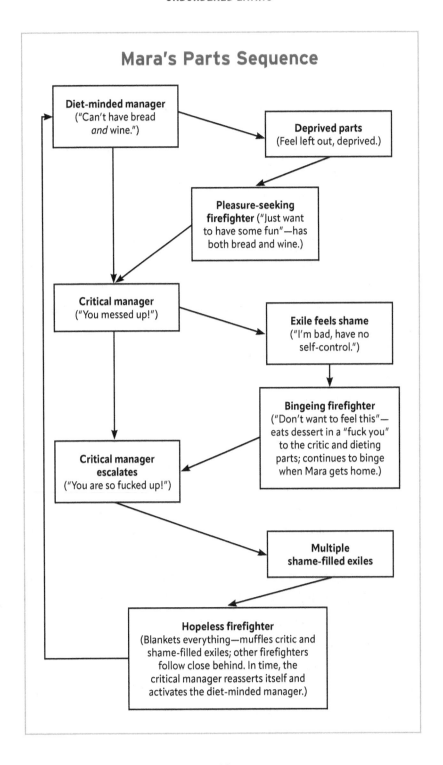

Mara's Parts Sequence

Diet-minded manager
("Can't have bread *and* wine.")

Deprived parts
(Feel left out, deprived.)

Pleasure-seeking
firefighter ("Just want
to have some fun"—has
both bread and wine.)

Critical manager
("You messed up!")

Exile feels shame
("I'm bad, have no
self-control.")

Bingeing firefighter
("Don't want to feel this"—
eats dessert in a "fuck you"
to the critic and dieting
parts; continues to binge
when Mara gets home.)

Critical manager
escalates
("You are so fucked up!")

Multiple
shame-filled exiles

Hopeless firefighter
(Blankets everything—muffles critic and
shame-filled exiles; other firefighters
follow close behind. In time, the
critical manager reasserts itself and
activates the diet-minded manager.)

As Mara reflected on this sequence of interactions between her parts, she got clearer about why each of the protectors felt and acted the way it did. She realized the hopeless part gave her a break from the anxiety and shame that came from the criticism and from repeated cycles of restricting and bingeing. However, the hopeless part unwittingly compounded those painful feelings because it motivated other firefighters to soothe the exiles by eating food and isolating. This instigated a fresh round of shaming from the critical part, who once again blamed the firefighters for eating too much and not restricting. Like kids in a family who blame themselves when the parents are fighting, Mara's exiles felt increasingly anxious and ashamed.

Like all protectors, Mara's hopeless part was in a quandary. While it could acknowledge the limitations of its strategy, it wasn't ready to stop doing what it did because it didn't trust Mara's Self enough to take that risk. Therefore, she continued to focus her attention on the hopeless part in therapy and between sessions. Staying connected to the part between sessions was crucial to earning the hopeless part's trust. It had been accustomed to other parts of Mara and other people in her life disliking it or trying to cheer it up in an attempt to get it to feel more hopeful. Mara showed the part that she cared about it by checking in with it on a daily basis, staying curious about its experience, and not trying to get it to change.

After a few sessions dedicated to building trust between Mara's Self and the hopeless part, I asked her if she could ask it to share more about what it feared would happen if it didn't keep blending with her.

"It says it doesn't believe that I can handle the critic, says I've never been able to, that I just let it take over."

"Does it have a point?" I asked.

Mara nodded. "Yes, I've been realizing how the critic's always there, pretty much every time I put something in my mouth."

"The hopeless part hasn't had the experience of your being able to relate to the critical part from Self. Let the hopeless part know that if it gives you a chance, you can show it that you can relate to the critical part directly, without letting it take over. If at any point the hopeless part is concerned that the critic is taking over, it can always let you know."

Mara was quiet for a moment before responding, "It's skeptical but willing to try."

With that, Mara was able to shift her attention to the critical part. As is often the case, she discovered that the critical part had intentions that were similar to those of the hopeless part. While it took a very different approach, the critical part was also determined to help Mara feel less ashamed and chaotic. Also like the hopeless part, the critic unintentionally engendered what it was trying to prevent.

As Mara became more adept at tracking her critical part, she found it particularly helpful to engage in dialogues with it between sessions. Sometimes she wrote out the questions and responses to these dialogues, while other times she simply spoke aloud to her critical part when it presented itself. Instead of pushing it aside or arguing with it, she got curious about it and asked questions like "What are you worried will happen if you don't find fault with me right now?" "Who are you trying to protect by doing this?" and "What do you want me to know by telling me this?"

The more Mara demonstrated her commitment to tracking and pausing the critical part instead of letting it take over, the more the hopeless protector trusted her—and eased up on its desperation.

Eventually, the hopeless part became willing to more fully unblend because Mara did the following:

1. She helped the hopeless part feel seen and valued for how it had been trying to help.

2. She validated the hopeless part's anger at the Self for not being present in the past (i.e., for letting the critic and other protectors blend).

3. She tracked the sequence of interactions between the hopeless part and other parts of the system, pausing the critical part when it got activated so it didn't take over the way it had previously.

4. She helped the hopeless part get to know the positive intentions of the critical part.

5. She offered hope for a different outcome by reassuring the hopeless part that if it agreed to relax, Mara's Self could also negotiate with the restricting and bingeing parts and heal the exiles they were trying to protect.

Establishing a relationship with the hopeless and critical protectors allowed Mara to get to know more about the parts involved in the restrict-binge cycle in a way she'd never found possible before. Instead of finding fault with these polarized protectors, she got curious about how they were provoking each other and learned more about the exiles they were trying to protect. As you'll see in the next chapter, the process of healing the exiles, called *unburdening*, allowed these protectors to transform instead of temporarily easing up on their roles.

"It Will Only Make Me Feel Worse"

Many protectors resist unblending because when they've tried to do so in the past, another part has taken over. The protectors' lived experience is that when they've relaxed or been unable to do their job (e.g., when internal or external conditions have thwarted them), something bad has happened. We saw this with Mara's hopeless part, who historically found that whenever it took a break and Mara became more relaxed in her outlook, the critical part inevitably came in to shame her for not controlling her hungry and "rebellious" parts when they disregarded the latest diet or wellness plan. This criticism amplified the exiles' shame, which in turn reactivated the protectors involved in the restrict-binge cycle.

This was also true for Natalie's "superior" manager, who ridiculed the critical part for its concerns. The "superior" part helped Natalie feel strong, competent, and true to herself. When this part relaxed, it watched as Natalie blended with her appearance-focused critical part and got caught up in others' opinions. For this reason, it wasn't surprising when Natalie's "superior" part objected to learning more about the critical part. It registered its opposition by tightening the upper right side of her chest.

I asked Natalie if she was curious about the "superior" part's reaction.

She held up a finger to signal that she was connecting internally with the part. "It says that connecting with the critical part is only going to make me feel things I don't want to feel. It says it doesn't believe there's a way to be with this part without ending up feeling worse afterward. It says it's not worth going there."

She added, "Of course, the problem is that I *am* going there. I mean, all I can think about is the wedding, how bad I'm going to look, and why I'm not doing anything about it."

Here, Natalie was describing the limitations of her "superior" protector. No matter how hard it tried to shut down the appearance-focused, critical part, the critic kept up its stream of negative thoughts and predictions about what would happen at the wedding. In order for the "superior" part to consider relaxing back so Natalie could be with the critic, Natalie had to reassure the "superior" part that she could be with the critical part in a way that didn't leave other parts of her feeling bad.

I explained to Natalie, "Well, there's a big difference between blending with the critical part, which is what's been happening lately, and relating to it from your Self. Let the 'superior' part know that if it would be willing to let you be with the critical part, you can get to know it without it taking over. You can find out how it's been trying to help you by being critical, including which parts it's trying to protect by finding fault with you."

Reminding the "superior" part that there was a reason for the critic's behavior helped it soften a bit more. This was different from how the "superior" part and many other parts of Natalie had viewed the critic. In the therapy world and elsewhere, inner critics are commonly seen as obstacles to well-being that need to be challenged, overridden, or eliminated. People are often encouraged to *do something* when their critical parts blend with them—push the critical parts aside, reassure them, tell them off, or ignore them—to comfort the parts who feel shame, fear, or worthlessness.

It is for this reason that Natalie's "superior" part had spent decades trying to fend off the appearance-focused critic by ignoring it and focusing instead on reasons why Natalie should appreciate her body (e.g., for being so strong, for having children, for being able to play tennis). While these tactics successfully distanced the critical part in the short run, they required a fair amount of ongoing effort because they didn't work to disarm the critic whenever social events required Natalie to be more out in the world.

When Natalie asked the "superior" part if its strategies had been helpful, it acknowledged that its efforts worked until they didn't. Natalie explained, "That's when other parts—who can't tolerate how bad the critical part makes me feel—get busy by distracting me with work I need to do around the house, playing games on my computer, and snacking on cereal or chocolate even though I'm not really hungry."

Natalie reflected for a moment before adding, "And then that just makes the critical part even more critical."

Natalie's *clarity* about the critical protector and its relationship to other parts of her system indicated she had more access to her Self. Sharing this awareness with her "superior" part would likely help it become more open to relaxing back further so she could get to know the critic.

I related my understanding of what Natalie had just shared with me. "That makes sense. Up until this point, parts of you have pushed the critic aside or tried to block it out by doing something else. But it doesn't go away because it has its own reasons for doing what it does. Let the 'superior' part know you understand why it's concerned, but if it gives us a chance, we can get to know the critic in a way that will make a difference. See if it's willing to give it a try. It can always go back to doing what it usually does if it needs to."

"It says it's willing to experiment but it's very clear about not wanting to dwell on this if it's going to make me feel bad about myself."

"What do you say to it?"

"I understand why it feels this way. There are times when it—the critical part—can be brutal."

"Great, Natalie, let it know that we can work with the appearance-focused critic so it doesn't overwhelm you. Remind the 'superior' part that it can come back in if feels like that's happening. It will help to get all the parts who dislike or fear the critic to go somewhere comfortable while you get to know it better."

"They want to be in the park—by the lake," Natalie replied.

"Sounds good. As you shift your attention to the appearance-focused critic, how do you feel toward it?"

Natalie reflected for a moment before answering. "I'm trusting you when you tell me that it has a positive intention—because this part is like a sniper."

"Yes, I guarantee this part has its reasons for doing what it does. Maybe it can share why it's come in so forcefully in anticipation of the wedding and what it's afraid would happen if it didn't."

"This wedding is going to be huge. Something like 250 people are invited and there's something about being the mother of the bride—all the attention that will be on me—that just makes me feel so anxious. Whew, I can feel it right here [*pointing to her chest*]. It makes me feel like I can't take a full breath."

I stayed quiet to see what else emerged as Natalie focused on the fear.

She continued, saying, "This feels really bad, like all of a sudden I can't move, but also like I want to run at the same time, all of this adrenaline."

I understood now why Natalie's many protectors had been so busy distracting her from her internal experience much of the time. She was blending with an exile who was paralyzed with fear. As you learned in chapter 2, exiles are parts who are kept out of awareness so they don't upset other parts of the system or get hurt again by other people. As you'll see, Natalie's exile was experiencing fear and paralysis due to what happened in the past. These feelings were exacerbated when the part was subsequently exiled because she carried those feelings.

We had reached a pivotal juncture in Natalie's work. If her protectors agreed to remain unblended, she could show them how she could be with the exile in a new way. Instead of getting overwhelmed by the exile's fear and immobility, as she had in the past, she could ask it to not overwhelm the system with what it carried. If the exile agreed, the protectors would have the opportunity to observe how Natalie's Self could be with and heal the exile. Once that happened, they wouldn't feel compelled to re-exile this part as they'd done so often in the past.

As Natalie stayed *calm* and *curious* about the exile's experience, its sensations of immobility and panic eased a bit. It showed her where it was stuck in the past: at her aunt's wedding when she was six. The exile shared how excited she'd been to be the flower girl until the day of the wedding, when she became flooded with anxiety about walking down the aisle.

"I was so worried that I was going to do it wrong and there was so much going on, but I didn't feel I could ask anyone for help. Everyone was stressed out and busy. I ended up crying and not being able to move when it came time for me to walk down the aisle. I just remember my father being so angry at me. He shouted at me in front of everyone and told me I was ruining everything. No one said anything to me and I just felt frantic."

As Natalie listened to the exile's story, she felt a lot of compassion for this young part of herself. "I've often joked with people about this story, like it was funny that I basically failed in my duties as a flower girl, but I guess I—I mean parts of me—split off how horrible it was, how frightened and alone I felt. And how desperate I [*an exile*] felt about upsetting my father like that. I think the worst thing was that no one did anything to stop him."

Natalie continued to witness the exile until it felt like she fully understood what it had suffered. As she did, she learned how the critical protector had taken on her father's energy to prevent the exile from being hurt again. If the protector could get Natalie to conform to her father's expectations, he wouldn't find fault with her and would love her the way this exile and other parts of her had longed for him to.

Natalie's critical protector was relieved to give up her father's energy when it saw that Natalie could be with and heal the exile who was stuck in the past at her aunt's wedding. It was happy to shift its role to being a supporter of the exile—of the part of Natalie who was naturally shyer, the one who froze when she was a little girl.

"It Won't Make a Difference"

As we saw with Mara and Natalie, parts are in dynamic tension with each other. As one part goes to one extreme, other parts try to balance out the system by going to another extreme. This tendency toward homeostasis is the nature of all living systems. As parts unblend and you have more access to your Self, you can help your parts appreciate how each has something valuable to contribute to the larger system. This, in turn, helps to ease system-wide tension as relationships between parts become less polarized.

When protectors realize that they're on the same team, with a leader who is interested in the well-being of all of the parts, they become more willing to consider the risky business of shifting out of their roles. This was a major part of my work with Christina, a thirty-two-year-old woman who grew up in a tight-knit family in the suburbs. The youngest of four, she was adopted by a couple who already had three biological sons.

"My parents really wanted a girl and my brothers were excited to have a little sister."

She knew little about her birth parents aside from basic demographics, which she learned from the agency that handled the adoption.

"My birth mother was Puerto Rican and my biological father was White. They already had several children and were separated when I was conceived. The only other thing I know is that I was born prematurely and that my birth mother had gestational diabetes."

Christina described her adoptive mother, Gina, as warm and funny. "She was the type of mom everyone wanted to hang out with. She loved hearing what we were up to."

Christina shared that Gina was explicit about her intention to be a different parent than her own mother; Gina's mother was a single parent who worked long hours and wasn't able to spend much time with her children.

However, Christina shared that Gina's wish for closeness had been challenging. "Sometimes I don't want to share what's going on with her, either because I need some space to sort out how I'm feeling or because I know she doesn't really want to hear how I'm feeling. It can be very hard for her to accept it when I say I don't want to talk about something. She takes it as a reflection of how I feel about her."

One topic Christina worked hard to avoid with Gina was weight and health. "I know she means well—she worries about all of us—but I am so tired of her commenting about her weight, my weight, and all of her concerns about whether I could get diabetes and what that would mean for me."

Christina went on to explain that from the time she was little, she was one of the biggest girls in the class, weight-wise. Her classmates teased her for being larger and also for having darker skin, given her Puerto Rican heritage.

"I was in preschool and they had us draw pictures of our families. Some of the other kids made fun of me for looking different than the rest of my family."

As Christina reflected on her experience, she continued, saying, "I wanted to be like the other moms and daughters who looked like each other. But I couldn't talk about how I felt because it upset my mother so much when I got upset. So I mostly kept it to myself."

Christina related how people whose opinion meant a great deal to her, including her best friend's mother, would tell her how pretty she was and how much prettier she'd be if she was thinner. To help her "be healthier and lose some weight," Gina prepared food for her that was different from what she made for everyone else. For example, on nights when she made pizza "for the boys," Gina gave Christina a salad with a diet-brand, lower-calorie pizza that was nothing like the real thing. In turn, Christina started to sneak her brothers' "junk" food, hiding it in her bedroom to eat when she was alone.

Over the past couple of years, Christina had worked hard to develop a different relationship with food and her body. As she focused on healing the exiles who carried shame and fear about her body, she was able to help them unload a lot of the shame they had been carrying. However, she still noticed a part who frequently got activated when she was around people who harbored anti-fat beliefs and feelings. "That feeling of being okay plummets when I'm around them. I know they see me as disgusting, which probably sounds extreme, but I just know that's how they feel. I see how differently they treat me when I'm thinner. I start out feeling confident about myself, and then a part of me gets scared that they are judging me for not realizing how bad I look. I start to feel tense and get confused about what I really look like."

When Christina tracked what happened inside when she found herself having an upsetting conversation with her mother or others who held similar biases about size and health, she noticed the following sequence of parts:

1. She perceives judgment (in the form of indirect and direct comments or glances), which activates an exile who feels "I'm too big, I'm disgusting."

2. This, in turn, activates a firefighter who is angry about being judged and intruded upon.

3. A people-pleasing, minimizing part tries to neutralize the angry firefighter by explaining the other person's intentions (e.g., "She loves me and is just concerned about me," "She can't control herself").

4. At the same time, another protector tries to "figure out" the validity of the external judgment (e.g., "How fat *do* I look?" "Are they right that I shouldn't be eating what I'm eating?").

5. Another part attempts to distract from and remedy the exile's feeling of not being okay with affirmations (e.g., "I'm fine the way I am").

6. The exile feels more alone with its shame and confusion.

7. The angry firefighter ramps up its efforts to ward off the shame by getting furious (internally) with the manager who minimizes other person's "well-meaning" judgment.

8. A dissociative part takes over, like a circuit breaker, to disconnect Christina from the exile's pain, the pleasing part's minimization, the "figuring out" part's rumination regarding the validity of the external judgment, and the firefighter's escalating anger about all of it, especially the external judgments.

9. As the external judgment continues (e.g., her mother keeps asking "innocent" questions), a part feels despair about how Christina keeps abandoning herself to other people's judgments.

Until Christina tracked this sequence, she hadn't realized she was blending with a dissociative protector. Although this part successfully blocked out the painful thoughts and feelings of the other parts, it also exposed her to more harm, as it prolonged interactions with her mother and other people who held damaging ideas related to food and bodies. For example, Christina recounted a recent interaction at her parents' home where she didn't speak up or object when her mother kept asking questions about Christina's annual physical exam. After Christina left that day, she noticed parts who felt despairing and frustrated because she'd allowed her mother to do this to her once again.

When we explored the dissociative part's fears about what would happen if it didn't take over in moments like these, it shared that its biggest concern was that the angry firefighter would take over and hurt her mother's feelings.

"This part just wants to scream at her, 'Stop making comments about my body!'"

I asked Christina what the dissociative part feared would be so bad if that happened.

"Because I'm adopted, and also because I'm the only girl, my mother has a lot of feelings about our relationship, about how close we are. If I let her know I'm angry, she'll get hurt. Then I'll end up feeling worse and feel like I have to take care of her. It's not worth it. It ends up being so much more work for me."

I said, "That makes sense. But ask the dissociative part how it's been working for it to do what it does."

Christina shook her head. "Obviously not very helpful because I end up getting angry and lashing out at some point. Or I just stop wanting to have anything to do with her, which is also a problem."

"Let the dissociative part know that if it doesn't shut you down like this, we can get to know the part who's angry and the parts it's polarized with—the ones who are so worried about upsetting your mother. We can learn more about their concerns and help them trust you to speak for the angry firefighter so it doesn't have to lash out."

Over the course of the next couple of months, Christina paid attention to this cluster of parts. She learned more about the ones who feared upsetting her mother and, as they relaxed, she connected with the angry firefighter and validated its concerns. One evening, while at her parents' home for dinner, Gina suggested to Christina that she might also want to skip dessert since dinner was so "rich."

Christina noticed a spike of anger followed by an urge to get up and leave. When she noticed her mind starting to go blank, she paused the dissociative part and asked if it would be willing to hold off on disconnecting her so she could help the parts who were getting activated. She reminded the dissociative part that she could help the parts who were angry as well as the ones who worried about upsetting her mother. She let all the parts know that they would all be okay if that happened—that she could take care of them.

As the parts unblended and Christina had more access to her Self-energy, she listened to her angry firefighter. She then spoke for it instead of storming out or saying something hurtful. "I understand you have ideas about what would be best for me. I'd appreciate it if you didn't make comments about what I eat or about my body. It feels really bad to parts of me."

Christina's mother responded by becoming defensive. "I'm just looking out for you. I want you to be healthy, and I don't get why that's a problem for you."

Gina then abruptly left the room, leaving Christina with her father and one of her brothers.

Her brother said, "I don't understand why you can't just let it go. You know Mom is just concerned about you."

Christina let her father and brother know that Gina's obsession about weight and health had impacted her. "What Mom said and continues to say about my body and her own body has been harmful.

She's always talking about how many carbs she's eating, commenting on the 'tire around her waist,' or worrying about the size of her arms and whether or not they're 'toned.' When she made these comments as I was growing up, I started to observe and worry about the size of my own stomach and arms, constantly checking myself in the mirror to see what I looked like. Her 'problem areas' became my own, and I wouldn't have become so focused on my body if she hadn't continuously talked about her body, my body, and bodies in general."

Christina's brother, frustrated with her, left the room to comfort their mother. Her father was quiet for a moment before changing the subject. As Christina left her parents' house later that night, she noticed feeling a familiar mixture of guilt, anger, and hopelessness. On an intellectual level, she knew that that she was doing what she needed to do to establish different boundaries with her family, but experiences like the one she'd just had left her feeling despair about the likelihood of being successful.

"What would 'successful' look like to you?" I asked.

Christina replied, "For them to see how their comments are not okay, how they're disrespectful and not helpful."

"Given that definition of success, does it make sense to you why parts of you would feel despair?"

Christina nodded. "Yes, I don't see how that's ever going to happen. There's a part of me who feels so sad about that. It just wants them to accept me for who I am and not who they want me to be."

"Ask the part who feels angry and the one who feels guilty if they can give you some room to get to know the part who's so sad about them not accepting you as you are. Let's see if we can get to know and help this part, to get her out of where she's stuck in the past."

Like many clients, Christina got some pushback from the parts who felt despair about things changing. Up until this point, her efforts to establish self-protective boundaries with her family (and even with certain friends) had elicited defensiveness and judgment about her "sensitivity" as well as her beliefs about food and bodies. We had to spend a considerable amount of time with her protectors, who either wanted to ignore or minimize everything (her dissociative and people-pleasing protectors) or get furious and lash out (her angry firefighter).

As Christina got to know these protectors and the exile who felt unloved, she discovered another exile who had internalized Gina's fear about what might happen to her body if she gained weight. This was a turning point in Christina's recovery, one she could not have reached until she befriended the protectors who kept her from being aware of this young part. She realized the exile's fear caused parts of her to become anxious and confused when someone challenged her with their ideas about "healthy" food and her body. For example, this often happened when others suggested that Christina eliminate certain food groups so she wouldn't get diabetes, or when they insinuated that if she developed diabetes, it would be her fault for not taking better care of herself. With permission from her protectors, Christina was able to heal (unburden) the fearful exile, as well as the one who was sad about being a disappointment to her mother for many different reasons: for being fat, for being angry, for wanting more space, and more recently, for rejecting her notions of health and beauty.

Once she did this work, Christina was less likely to question herself for feeling confident or for making certain choices regarding food and movement. While her mother's comments about food and her health continued to make parts of Christina angry, she began trusting this anger as a signal that parts of her needed her to set a limit. Often, this involved changing the subject or making arrangements that protected her well-being (e.g., limiting her stays at her parents' home, bringing friends to family gatherings, renting a car to ensure that she could be flexible with her plans). While Christina did not feel she needed to cut off contact with her parents to take care of herself, other clients of mine have had to do this to protect their parts.

As you've learned in this chapter, it's almost always the case that you can't get to know your exiles without negotiating with the protective parts who have worked hard to keep them out of your awareness. When you don't blend with, override, or fight with these protectors, and instead learn about the fears they have about easing up on or letting go of their ways of coping, they will relax back and allow you to do the deeper work of unburdening exiles. The following chapter will focus on this transformational next step.

Chapter 5

Unburdening: Releasing Limiting Feelings and Beliefs

"Each of us carries legacy burdens inherited from our families and cultures, and each of us also accrues plenty of personal burdens along the way. [We begin] with unloading those burdens, and that sets the stage for the most important lesson of all—finding out who we really are."

–Richard Schwartz

Even when you're tired of dieting or wishing you had a different body, and even when you're clear about how messed up it is that you've been taught to manage or hide your body, it's likely that parts of you keep getting caught up in feeling bad about or trying to change it. As appealing as it is to imagine a world in which you are encouraged to treat your own and others' bodies with compassion, it's not the world you live in, and parts of you are well aware of that.

As you learned in the last chapter, protectors have their reasons for resisting letting go of their protective strategies. They've watched as other protectors took over and ate in a way that made you feel uncomfortable or got you to embark on another diet or cleanse, or your exiles flooded your system with their pain. They may have seen how you and other people have been treated when you stopped "trying" (whatever that means!).

Until you heal the parts of yourself who hold shame and fear about yourself and your body, your protectors will remain on guard to prevent you from getting hurt or feeling the exiles' pain again. They need some help from you to trust that within you is a core wisdom, your Self, that can be relied on to handle the internal and external disruptions that will naturally occur when they agree to shift out of their roles.

With some infusion of Self-energy (from your Self or from that of a trusted friend, community member, or therapist), your protectors will typically relax and open up some space so you can go to and heal the burdened parts of your system. Through a series of healing steps that culminate in what IFS refers to as *unburdening*, these parts can let go of their limiting beliefs and feelings so they revert back to their inherently valuable, joyful, open nature.

In this chapter, you'll learn how the IFS model facilitates the unburdening process and discover how the release of painful beliefs heals the exiles and liberates protectors to do things that are more gratifying and fulfilling.

Unlearning versus Unburdening

Burdens are extreme feelings and false beliefs that parts of you took on, most commonly when you were young or vulnerable. As I discussed in chapter 2, they may have come from experiences that you personally went through, or they may have been transmitted by other people in your environment or family or cultural lineage.

The burdens that get transmitted about bodies have been likened to corsets (Piran, 2017) and shame sweaters (Taylor, 2018)—analogies that align well with how IFS views these constraints: as feelings and beliefs that attach to parts but are not intrinsic to them. As you help parts to release these burdens, they revert back to their unselfconscious and often playful states.

However, as you've seen, this is easier said than done. It can be difficult for your parts to trust that it's safe to let go of burdens related to food and your body so you can reconnect with your core wisdom. As much as some parts of you are outraged and want to reject what's been foisted on you by the dominant culture, other parts of you are afraid to do so. They're the parts who continue to count calories or carbs, the ones who grab parts of your body saying, "If only I could get rid of this."

This is why liberating yourself is so challenging. You can't simply unlearn what you've been taught. Your burdened parts won't be swayed by cognitive interventions, at least not for very long, because these parts are stuck in the past when they got hurt. Logic simply won't access the brain regions with which these parts are associated (Anderson et al., 2017).

Instead, healing is a relational process that involves helping these burdened parts trust that they're not alone now and that you care about what they've gone through (and are going through) and what they fear. They need your help to see that you're a capable adult who has the wisdom to take care of them without resorting to punitive or limiting protective strategies. Vanessa and Leo's experiences will help you get a sense of how the unburdening process works.

When What Worked in the Past No Longer Works

Vanessa was a forty-year-old Black woman who came to me for a consultation at the urging of a friend, who was concerned about her preoccupation with food and her weight. A cybersecurity specialist who was married with two young children, she described feeling depleted by the many demands on her time and energy. What concerned her the most was her inability to lose the weight she'd gained during her two pregnancies. "Already overweight" prior to having her daughters, she was increasingly distressed by how she felt in her clothes and the fact that many of them no longer fit. She related that while she tried not to think about it, she felt "pretty desperate" about being "stuck at this weight and in this body."

Vanessa had met her husband, Kevin, at the gym five years earlier. They were big fans of Muay Thai, a mixed martial art that involved rigorous physical conditioning. It was an activity that kept them connected and helped Vanessa decompress. Now, however, it took a backseat to the many responsibilities related to raising the kids and keeping up with their demanding jobs. Vanessa's husband tried to comfort her by reassuring her how much he loved her body.

Vanessa told me, "It's obviously better that he says that, but it's like I can't really take that in. What else is he going to say?"

Here, Vanessa was blended with a critical manager who, along with other self-reliant managers, often led the way. These hard-working parts had helped her navigate competitive school and work environments as well as difficult family dynamics. Focused on school and athletics, these high-achieving parts distracted Vanessa from her parents' chronic conflict and helped her secure a partial scholarship to college. They also helped her excel at demanding jobs, especially her current position at an investment bank.

Despite their obvious advantages, Vanessa's managers' high standards could be exhausting and inflexible in the face of changes, like the ones she recently experienced when she had two children in quick succession. These protectors experienced a kind of identity crisis when she fell into a postpartum depression that wouldn't lift. The demands on Vanessa's time and energy thwarted the protectors' habitual strategies, which were to wall off her vulnerability, helping her endure whatever she needed to get through. Vanessa felt anxious and self-conscious in a way she hadn't in years.

When she tried to tell herself that it was normal to struggle in the ways she was, a critical part ridiculed her for feeling anxious and depressed and for not losing weight. It didn't understand why she couldn't eat less and find some way to get to the gym. This critical part felt validated by her doctor's concern about her weight as well as what she observed among her friends, who were similarly committed to managing their bodies and their lives.

Self-Energy Disrupts Culturally Driven Shame and Blame

It was only because she was so depressed and upset by her inability to lose weight that Vanessa agreed to try IFS at the suggestion of a friend who had found this therapy helpful. Her friend's self-compassion regarding her own body and emotional struggles was a relieving counterpoint to Vanessa's distress.

At the outset of our work together, I explored Vanessa's feelings about meeting with me given that I am a White woman. She expressed concern about how well I would understand her, both because I was White and because she knew I wasn't pro-dieting. I let her know I understood why parts of her would be concerned about my being White and that if at any time she felt too vulnerable, or if parts of her had questions or concerns, I would welcome slowing things down so we could address them. I added that while my perspective is that dieting is corrosive, I would not tell her what to do but, rather, help her get curious about her own system.

In these early sessions, Vanessa was often blended with and spoke from the vantage point of a critical manager who was upset by her inability to stop feeling depressed and "get it together." I suggested that instead of trying to push past or reassure this part, as her husband and family had been doing, that we get to know more about it and what it was trying to do for her.

She shook her head with frustration and said, "I just need to stop navel-gazing and move on."

I responded, "The part who's speaking now, that's the one we'd like to get to know. That's the part you've been hearing from a lot lately?"

She nodded. "Pretty much all of the time. I'm so tired of feeling this way."

"I bet. It sounds like it's been really hard. If you're open to it, I can help you get to know this part and see what it's trying to do for you."

"My friend Naomi told me you were able to help her, so I'm willing to try. Though, if I'm honest, a part of me wants to say, 'Have at it, but you're not going to be able to get anywhere with it.'"

"I know you said it's new for you to speak with a therapist, so I want to acknowledge the parts who are willing to give this a chance right now. I'm also hearing you have a part who feels quite skeptical that this will help and another part who is really tired of the one who criticizes you. Let them know that if they give us a chance, we can get to know this part who can be so harsh and help it. Ask inside and see if they'd like that—don't think about it, just notice what comes back from that place in your body."

"Okay," Vanessa replied as she closed her eyes and focused her attention inside. After a long pause, she opened her eyes and said, "I'm not getting much, like no words or anything, but I do notice feeling quieter inside."

Understanding this to reflect that Vanessa was more open (had more access to Self), I said, "Great. See if you can find the part who's so critical of you for being depressed and unable to get it together. Where do you notice that part in or around your body?"

"It's mostly here," she said, pointing to just over her heart.

"As you focus on the sensation, how do you feel toward it?"

Vanessa took a deep breath and said, "It makes sense to me. I feel like this is pretty basic self-care. It shouldn't be this hard."

I responded, "This is the part we want to get to know and help, the one who keeps saying, 'This is pretty basic.' See if it would be willing to separate from you a little so you can be with it rather than being dominated by it."

"I'll try," Vanessa replied, closing her eyes to focus on the part. "Okay, it's giving me a little room."

"Great. Can you see this part, or do you just sense it?"

"I don't see it. I can sense it, though. It's impatient."

"Are you open to hearing from it?"

Vanessa nodded.

I continued, saying, "Let this part know you're interested in knowing why it feels impatient."

Vanessa responded, "It's upset about how out of control things feel, how I'm not doing *anything* very well."

"As you hear this, how are you feeling toward it?"

Vanessa shook her head. "This part is pretty frantic. I would like to help it feel better."

"Let it know that you'd like to help. See how it reacts to your compassion."

Vanessa replied, "It's a little calmer."

"Okay, great. See if it can tell you more about its belief that you're not doing anything very well."

"It's saying that I'm not focused at work, I'm stressed out all the time, and I'm not doing anything to take care of myself. This part is really, like *really*, concerned about my body and how I'm not doing anything about it."

"Does the part sense that you're with it right now? How close can you get to it in your mind's eye?"

Vanessa closed her eyes. "Again, I can't see it, but I can sense its energy. It's very tense and young, around eleven or twelve."

"Let it know you're interested in knowing more about why it's so upset."

"She's mad at me for being so depressed and not doing the things I should be doing—things that make me feel better, like getting to the gym. If I were doing that, I'd be less stressed out and I would be losing this weight."

"Do you know why she's so worried about your weight?"

Vanessa closed her eyes to focus on the part. After a minute, she opened her eyes and said, "It makes her feel out of control, like I'm not put together. Nothing fits, and it's just going to get worse. It's like I can't control anything—my moods, my body."

"So is this what she does for you? Tries to help you get in control?"

Vanessa nodded affirmatively.

"Ask her to let you know more about her role of trying to help you get in control. Maybe you can start by asking her how long she's been doing this."

Vanessa was quiet for a few minutes before responding. "For a long time, since around the time I was twelve or thirteen."

"Ask her if she can tell you what led her to take on this role."

As Vanessa focused her attention on this part, it related how her parents got divorced when she was twelve and her father moved in with a woman whose two sons were a couple of years older than Vanessa. The boys made fun of her developing body and did things to embarrass her. Most of this happened out of earshot of the adults.

Vanessa said, "When my dad and the boys' mother did overhear some of what the boys were saying, they chalked it up to typical adolescent brother-sister dynamics."

I asked Vanessa what else the critical part had to say about that time, and she said she couldn't rely on any of the adults to help with what she was going through.

"They didn't understand why I was so upset. It was so difficult for them that I couldn't just deal. Whenever I had to go over to my dad's house, I spent a lot of time in my room eating by myself. I didn't want them watching me eat—they were always on me for what I was eating— and it was the only thing that helped me feel better. But then I started gaining weight and that really upset everyone."

Vanessa described how the critical manager emerged at that time. "It got me to stop dwelling on how I was feeling and do things that would help me feel more put together, like watching what I ate and exercising."

I asked Vanessa how she felt toward the critical part.

She opened her eyes and said, "I didn't realize how bad it feels and how hard it's been working."

Appreciating a Critical Protector's Contribution to Earn Its Trust

Validating the critical part's positive intentions was eye opening for Vanessa. Parts of her felt exhausted by the critic's demands. They were angry with it for how it made them feel and hopeless about getting it to stop. As Vanessa got to know the critic and how it tried to help her, the parts who hated the critic softened a bit. This gave Vanessa more access to her Self. This, in turn, allowed Vanessa to get even more curious about the critical part, more respectful of how hard it had been working on her behalf. She realized how determined the critical part had been to keep her from eating in a way that elicited her family's (and others') disapproval and to alleviate her exiles' loneliness and sadness.

Vanessa continued, saying, "I appreciate how it's been trying to help me. When I consider how young this part is, I feel bad that it had to deal with all of that."

"Let the part know you feel for it and see how it responds."

"I can see this part more clearly now. She relaxes a little when I let her know I appreciate how much she's had to deal with. Those were not easy people to grow up with."

"Vanessa, see if this part can tell you what she's afraid would happen if she didn't work so hard to control what you do."

Vanessa took a minute before responding. "She's afraid I'll stay depressed, keep overeating, and gain more weight."

"If she knew that we could get to know and help the exiles she protects, the ones who are depressed and need soothing, would she have to keep working so hard to keep it together?"

"She doesn't see how that's possible, but she says she'd obviously prefer that."

"Let her know that this is what we're going to do, with her help. If she can give us a little room and ease up on criticizing you, we can get to know the vulnerable parts she's been trying to take care of."

"She says she's willing to try it, but if I gain weight that's a deal breaker."

With this comment I understood the protector's bottom line: She would consider relaxing her criticism to a certain degree, but only if it didn't result in Vanessa gaining weight. I understood that I needed to stay curious about this concern. Otherwise, I risked alienating this protector and more or less inviting it to dig its heels in.

Knowing we needed to explore this part's fears about weight gain, I said, "We're going to want to learn more about why she feels that way too—why that would be so upsetting. For now, though, let her know you appreciate her willingness to let you get to know her and what she's been trying to do for you."

Over the next few sessions, we continued to learn more about how hard Vanessa's critical manager had worked to keep her exiles out of awareness—by focusing squarely on what Vanessa could do better. As Vanessa got to know it and other managers better, she realized how much energy it took to be so self-sufficient, vigilant, and self-critical. She realized how these strategies activated firefighters like the eating part and choked off the playful, more vulnerable parts of her system, the ones who had been more easygoing and curious before they got hurt. You'll hear more about Vanessa's healing later in this chapter.

When What Happened in the Past Won't Stay in the Past

Leo was a gay man in his late twenties who was referred to me by his Alcoholics Anonymous (AA) sponsor. Like Vanessa, parts of Leo carried burdens that made it difficult to hold onto the positive feedback he received from friends, colleagues, and especially men in whom he was interested. Whether it was his sense of humor, intelligence, or appearance, he minimized or forgot the good things he heard and focused instead on the negative. He couldn't reconcile what he heard with how he felt inside, which was chronic anxiety about being judged, rejected, or fired.

Leo identified as gay to friends and colleagues but not to his parents, who had immigrated to the United States from Italy when they were in their early twenties and remained ensconced in an Italian community in Boston.

He was particularly worried that his father would be disappointed in him. "I've never been who he wanted me to be, except for in school. It's a total cliché—he loves sports, I hate sports. He's extroverted, the mayor-about-town kind of guy, I like to read and do things more on my own. We're just completely different. He would not be okay with me being gay. My younger sister is really the only one I ever talk to in my family, and she says she thinks he doesn't want to know."

Leo identified his temperamental mismatch with his father as an obvious source of self-doubt and, at times, serious depression. He often felt inferior to and rejected by his older brother, Nick, who was athletic and popular and, as Leo believed, favored by their father.

While Leo intellectually understood these issues had to impact his self-esteem, he couldn't understand why he felt as "shaky" in himself as he did. "People find me funny, fun to be with, attractive. But once I like someone, I can't hold onto that sense of myself. All of a sudden I find myself feeling insecure, like I'm not enough."

He described the pain he felt about his breakup with a boyfriend who ended their relationship. "He got tired of my constant questioning about what he was doing—and whom he was seeing. I just couldn't get it out of my head that he wasn't as attracted to me and was going to leave."

He described several relationships that followed a similar trajectory. After a couple of months where things felt good, parts of him started to get anxious about the relationship ending. Leo employed several strategies to cope with his insecurity. A vigilant manager scanned other people for signs they might be losing interest while a people-pleasing part worked hard to anticipate the other person's needs. Another manager pushed him to go to the gym so he could lose weight and become more muscular. Although he was in his late twenties, parts of Leo were already preoccupied with what it meant to age as a gay man.

He told me, "It will be even harder for me to meet someone the older I get."

Leo also had a critical manager who ridiculed the anxious parts and a firefighter who drank to take the edge off and get a break from both the anxious parts and the hardworking managers.

Following his recent breakup, Leo started to drink more heavily as his firefighter looked for ways to numb and soothe the exiles who were frantic about the end of the relationship. During a particularly bad drinking binge, he had a frightening experience that prompted him to go to an AA meeting. He chose a meeting for gay men close to where he lived, which was an eye-opening experience. Leo resonated with the loneliness and self-recrimination he heard, especially from other men who also came from patriarchal, close-knit, religiously conservative families like his own.

The Importance of Community Support

Leo's experience underscores the importance of connection and community in providing protectors with the support and hope they need to unblend. As Niva Piran (2020) states, "You can do therapy but that power of belonging to a community that shares important characteristics with you and shows you how you can be powerful and belong in a very equitable way to the community is a transforming experience."

As Leo spent time with other men who knew firsthand the pain of growing up gay in this culture and in his ethnic group, parts of him felt seen and understood in a way they had never been before. Leo's harsh critic relaxed when he heard from these men, who also drank to block out loneliness and shame and whose low self-worth sometimes led them to hold onto relationships that were imbalanced or outright abusive.

"Some guys talked about the same panic in relationships that led them to do some of what I was doing—drinking, hooking up with other guys to feel better about myself, being with guys who weren't good for me."

As Leo's critic softened in this resonance, he felt more compassion (a reflection of Self-energy) toward similar parts in his own system.

And as Leo continued to attend meetings, he realized how much his drinking related not only to his abandonment anxiety but more fundamentally to how he felt about his sexuality and the shame that parts of him carried.

He said, "I know it might seem strange, but I wasn't aware of how bad I felt about myself because I'm gay. I'd kind of split my life into two different realities, the one I live here in the city and the one I have with my family back home. It's been pretty easy to keep things separate."

Because of this divide, Leo struggled with coming out to his family and also felt shame about having such a hard time doing so, since most of his gay friends had come out years earlier. By listening to others whose recoveries Leo admired, he found himself questioning the beliefs that parts of him had taken on about himself and all the ways they had been desperate to hide what they'd been taught was unacceptable. He felt clearer about how wrong it was that he'd been made to feel this way.

With the support of his sponsor, Leo stopped drinking. While he felt better in some ways without his alcohol-using firefighter, he felt his anxious and sad parts more acutely. His sponsor suggested he might find individual IFS therapy helpful to heal these vulnerable parts of his system, who were the primary drivers of much of his drinking.

Offering Hope for a Different Possibility

Leo decided to follow up on his sponsor's recommendation to give individual IFS therapy a try because the inspiration and self-compassion he felt at meetings quickly dissipated once he was alone. He also had a hard time identifying some of his beliefs and feelings as extreme and not objective facts.

For example, he discounted his concerns about his appearance and aging as "par for the course for a gay guy living in New York City. A lot of people I know are much worse about this than I am."

In Leo's initial session with me, he related frustration at how insecure he often felt in romantic relationships and sometimes at work. A critical manager hated how needy his anxious parts felt about getting others' approval and blamed these parts for being "too much" when things didn't work out. Several other managers teamed up to help Leo distract from his exiles' neediness and anxiety. These included an appearance-focused part and a manager Leo referred to as his "keep busy" part.

While Leo didn't consider his preoccupation with exercise and "clean eating" problematic, parts of him felt exhausted by how much time he spent at the gym and on meal planning. These tired parts also resented how little time they had to relax when his "keep busy" part not only allied with the appearance-focused part to get him to the gym but also signed up for drawing and language classes to help him avoid feeling lonely and anxious at night after work.

At the start of treatment, Leo wanted to get rid of his anxiety and wasn't all that curious about what was keeping him feeling that way. I offered that if his critical manager who was intolerant of his anxious parts would be willing to relax and open space, we could help the "keep busy" part who was working so hard to keep the anxiety at bay. Once we did that, we could heal his anxious parts so they didn't feel so needy. After several sessions, Leo's critical manager agreed to give us some room to do this work.

I asked Leo how he felt toward the "keep busy" part who kept him constantly on the go.

He said, "It's almost like trying to outrun the feelings. It's exhausting."

He also noticed the tension in his arms and chest. While some parts liked how productive this protector was, other parts hated how driven it made Leo feel much of the time. I asked him if he could ask these parts to relax a bit so he could get to know the "keep busy" part better. He nodded.

"Okay, great. Shift your attention to the part who keeps you moving and let it know you'd like to get to know it."

He nodded to indicate he was focusing on the part.

"See what it wants you to know about what it's trying to do by keeping you busy."

"It says it keeps me feeling like I'm being productive and doing things that are interesting to me and other people. It makes me feel like I'm moving in the right direction and that no matter what happens, I've got something going on."

"How do you feel toward this part as you hear this?"

"I appreciate how it is working to do this for me even though it can be exhausting."

"Let it know that and see how it responds to your appreciation."

"I feel less tension here," Leo said, pointing to his chest.

"It's easing a bit as you acknowledge its intention?"

Leo nodded. I followed by asking him to ask the part what it feared would happen if it stopped doing so much.

"It doesn't like that idea very much. There have been times when I haven't been able to do what this part gets me to do, like when I've been sick or with my family, and I start to get anxious. It says I wouldn't know what to do with myself. I might start drinking."

"So just thinking about easing up a little brings up some anxiety. It's afraid you wouldn't know what to do with the anxious parts who fear being rejected or abandoned?"

"Yes."

"I imagine you understand why it fears that. There have been times when the anxious parts have taken over?"

"Yes, and that's when I end up doing all kinds of things I shouldn't. Like checking to see if the guy I'm interested in is online or texting him late at night—which makes him feel like I'm checking on him, which of course I am—or eating something. Now that I'm not drinking, eating something to try to feel better has become more of a thing for me. Even though I know it's going to make me feel like shit like ten minutes later."

"So it sounds like you understand why this part is worried. Is this a long-standing pattern?"

Leo nodded.

"Okay, so let the 'keep busy' part know you understand that it's been trying to help you, and ask if it likes having to do this for you."

"It says it's better than the alternative."

"That makes sense. But ask it this: If it knew you could help the anxious parts so they didn't feel so alone, would it like to be able to do something else? Something it would like to do more?"

"It doesn't believe it's possible. When I'm in that place, the feelings are so intense."

"Let it know you hear that; you get that it believes the anxiety is too intense for you to handle. Leo, can you ask this part how old it thinks you are?"

Leo mulled this over for a minute before saying, "It feels like I'm nine or ten."

"Okay, let it know how old you really are."

"It's a little surprised."

"Let it know you understand it doesn't trust you to be able to help your anxious parts, but if it gives you a chance, you can show it that times have changed. See if it would agree to relax and give you some space to get to know the parts who are so anxious and insecure. It can always step back in if it feels like it needs to."

"It's willing to try."

IFS Healing Steps

The deep respect and appreciation that IFS holds for all parts is a powerful balm for even the most seemingly intractable or extreme protectors and the parts who fear or dislike them. Protective parts, who are typically over their heads doing jobs they don't enjoy or feel equipped to do, become more open to shifting out of their roles once they trust that the Self understands the risks involved and provides enough hope for a different outcome. When the protectors agree to give space, the Self can go to and heal the exiles, which frees the protectors from their constraining roles. Healing the exiles occurs through a series of actions known as the *IFS Healing Steps*:

- Witnessing
- Retrieval
- Unburdening
- Invitation
- Integration
- Following up

The following case vignettes briefly illustrate the healing steps. For a more thorough discussion of the unburdening process, please see *Internal Family Systems Therapy* (Schwartz & Sweezy, 2020).

Witnessing

As Leo befriended his "keep busy" manager, it gave him permission to get to know one of the anxious exiles it worked to protect. Leo focused his attention inside to locate the exile who felt insecure so he could *witness* what this part had experienced in the past.

"Where do you notice the anxious part?" I asked.

"I feel it here, in the pit of my stomach. It's an awful feeling, like the bottom is dropping out. This part feels totally alone, like he's a tiny speck in a huge void. No one can help him."

"How do you feel toward him as you hear this?"

"I feel sorry for him. But I don't like feeling like this."

"Of course not, so ask the parts who don't like feeling like this to let us help the anxious part so he doesn't have to keep feeling like this. Let them know we can ask the anxious part not to overwhelm you with his feelings. We can just listen to him and get to know his experience."

Here, I addressed a fear common to protectors, that if they open space so the exile can be *witnessed*, the exile will overwhelm the system with all of its painful feelings, memories, and sensations. I reassured Leo and his protectors that we could be with whatever the exile wanted us to know. Also, if it did begin to feel like too much for the protectors, I would speak to the exile directly and ask it to dial down its intensity a bit—enough so the protectors wouldn't be scared.

"Okay, give me a second." Leo closed his eyes for a moment. "Okay, they [*the protectors who disliked the anxious part*] backed off."

"Great. Do you have a sense of how old the anxious part is?"

"He's nine or ten. He's alone in his bedroom. His dad is really pissed that he doesn't want to go to football practice. His dad is the coach and he's upset because he says he did it for me and I'm not into it. He's saying I should be more like my brother." Here, Leo is speaking as the exile.

"How are you feeling toward this part as you hear this?" By asking this question, I am hoping Leo will unblend from the exile and relate to it from his Self.

"I feel for him. It felt awful for him to make me bad for not wanting to go."

Leo was now able to witness what had happened to this young part of himself in the past, where it remained stuck.

"Let him know you feel for him and that you want to know whatever it is he wants to share about that time and how hard it was."

Leo took a deep breath and said, "This happened all the time. I could hear my parents talking about me in their bedroom. My dad would say there was something wrong with me, that I didn't want to play sports or do other things that he felt I should want to do."

"Ask the boy to share whatever he needs to share until he feels like you get how bad it was."

"He was jealous of his brother for being good at sports. He was always my father's favorite."

"Leo, how close are you to the boy in your mind's eye?"

"Not very. I'm across the room from him. He's curled up on the bed, with the sheet over his head."

"Ask him if he'd like you to come closer."

"He's okay with me sitting next to the bed. He says he's not sure about me yet."

"That makes sense. He doesn't know you very well, isn't that right?"

Leo nodded his head. "I haven't really known about this part. I've spent a lot of time trying to get away from him."

"Okay, so let him know that it makes sense to you that he wouldn't know you and that he might have some feelings about how you allowed other parts to keep you away from him. See how he responds."

"He pays attention to me when he hears that. He's not moving or looking at me, but I can tell he's listening."

"Okay, as you're with him at the side of the bed, ask if there's anything more he wants you to see, sense, hear, or know about what he experienced at that time."

"He says he felt so sad, like he really wanted to be close to his dad, but he was always disappointing him. There was always something he couldn't get right."

"See if there's more he wants you to know about always being disappointing."

"I was shy and hated being the center of attention. My dad was always that guy who would make everyone laugh. Everyone wanted to be around my dad. And my brother was like that too. He always had tons of friends. I had friends, but they were like me—quieter, less outgoing. My father was always saying things like 'Lighten up, what's wrong with you?'"

"How do you feel toward the boy as you're hearing this?"

"I feel bad for him. He was really depressed, really sad that his father didn't like him."

"Let him know you get how sad he was about that. See if there's more he wants you to know. We want to be sure he feels that you *really* get how bad it was."

"He's reminding me of the time my father made fun of me after a game, in front of everyone. My dad was frustrated with me because I wasn't paying attention and I dropped a ball I should have caught. Everyone laughed as he imitated me. Even I did, because he was funny, but I was mortified, and deep down, I was so hurt. I just couldn't understand how my father could do that. It was awful."

Leo's voice caught in his throat.

"Is it okay to feel this much?" I asked.

When Leo nodded, I told him, "Let him know you're with him and see what else he wants you to know."

This last question was designed to assess how much access Leo had to his Self in this moment. To the degree that he could be with the exile's experience without getting overwhelmed, his exile would feel held by the Self and not dropped once again. His protector would be more trusting of Leo's Self to handle the exile's pain without its help.

"He's telling me more about how alone he felt and how much he wanted to be close to my father. My mother always told me how much my father loved me but I—this part—just didn't believe it. I mean, I know he's proud of me and I know he cares . . ."

Leo's lapse into reframing his father's behavior alerted me to the presence of another part, one who was loyal to his father. If Leo blended with this part, the exile's connection to the Self would be severed and he would be alone with his pain. I voiced my concern.

"It sounds like a part who's defending your father is coming in right now. Is that right? Take a moment to check."

"Yes, it's another part who's saying my father does care."

"Okay, Leo, let that part know you hear it and ask if would sit off to the side so you could stay with the boy who didn't feel loved. How do you feel toward the boy now?"

Here, I was checking to make sure Leo was able to unblend from the part who felt loyal to his father. I wanted to ensure that Leo's Self was connecting with his little boy. His response affirmed that this was the case.

"I care about him; I feel sad that he feels so alone, and I want to help him."

"Okay, let him know that and see how he reacts."

"He's so sad. But he feels that I care about him and he likes that."

"Great. Is there anything else he wants you to know about what it was like for him back there?"

Leo shook his head as if to say no, then paused. "He wants me to know that he wasn't just sad, he was scared. It was really frightening to feel like my father didn't like me. And it certainly didn't get any easier when I realized I was attracted to guys."

Here, another part was chiming in to add further detail about why parts of Leo felt disliked by his father. Wanting to stay with the exile's experience, I thanked that part and let it know that we would talk to it too, at a later time. I returned to the target exile and reiterated what it related about being sad and scared.

I asked Leo, "What do you say to him?"

"I understand that and I'm sorry he feels so bad about himself. I've always hated this part because I feel like he's fucked up every relationship I have with his anxiety."

"Parts of you disliked him too," I said, distinguishing parts of Leo from his Self.

"Yes, they've blamed him, believing if only he wasn't so needy, things would have worked out."

"What do you want to say to him now?"

"I'm sorry I let that happen, that I let them make him the problem."

"How is that for him to hear?"

"It makes him cry. He just says again how hard it's been. He's okay with me being next to him. I'm putting my arm around him."

Retrieval

At this point in the process, Leo was making a repair, acknowledging how the Self had failed to protect the exile in the past and allowed it to get hurt. This acknowledgment helped the part trust Leo's Self more and set the stage for the next healing step in IFS, which is referred to as *retrieval*. At this pivotal juncture, the Self joins the exile in the *time and place* where it got hurt. The Self continues to learn about what happened until the part feels fully witnessed for how bad the past was. Once at this point, the part is usually ready to leave that time and come into the present. The Self offers to help the part by intervening—protecting the part in the way it needed at the time, an optional aspect of the retrieval process known as a *redo*.

"That's really great, Leo. Be with him in the way he needed someone to be with him at that time. Ask him what else he needs for you to know, see, do, or say for him back there."

"He wants someone to stop my father when he's mocking me. To pull him aside and make him stop."

"Can you do that for him?" I asked.

Leo nodded. "I just told him to cut it out, that the boy was doing his best and that it hurts him so much for his dad to make fun of him."

"What is that like for the boy?" I continued.

"It's a big relief for him to see someone stand up for him."

"See if there's anything else he'd like you to do or say for him."

"He is shaking his head. He's leaning against me and just saying he wants to get out of there."

"Okay, great. Ask him where he'd like to be with you."

"He just wants to be with me where I live. He wants to go to the dog park with me."

"Great. Is he there with you now?"

"Yes, he feels calmer, less sad. It's big for him to feel like I don't hate him, that I see him and I really like him."

"That's really great. Let him know that, if he likes, he can unload that belief, or any other beliefs and feelings he got from that time."

"He says he wants to let go of the idea that there's something wrong with him. He knows that he's a good kid. He was just different from my dad and my brother."

"That's right, just different."

Unburdening

When parts feel fully witnessed by the Self for what they experienced, they are typically willing to leave the past and come into the present, where they can release the extreme beliefs and feelings they've been carrying. As you've learned, the latter process is known as *unburdening*.

As Leo's exile felt seen and understood by the Self, he realized the belief he had been holding for so long—that he was defective for not being like his father and brother—was mistaken. With this clarity and the loving support of his Self, the exile now felt ready to let go of this painful and limiting burden.

In IFS, we ask parts how they would like to release their burdens, which typically involves releasing it with the help of one of the five elements or anything else the part can think of that would facilitate its healing.

"Ask him what he'd like to release this belief to—light, water, wind, earth, fire, or anything else."

"He says he wants to give it up to the wind."

"Okay, Leo, have him notice where he carries the belief that there's something wrong with him in or around his body. Then help him let the wind take it away."

Leo remained with his eyes closed for a minute or so before speaking. "The wind pulled the belief out of all the places he was holding it in his body—his stomach, his heart, and his chest."

I had him check to make sure the boy had released it all to the wind.

"Yep, it's all out. And so is the shame and anxiety that went with that belief. He let go of that too."

"That's fantastic, Leo."

Invitation

After a part has unburdened, it's helpful to ask it what it would like to invite into its body to take the place of what was released. This represents the next step in the IFS healing process—the *invitation*— which is what I encouraged Leo to do after the exile released its burdens to the wind. "Ask him if there's anything he'd like to invite into his body in place of what he unburdened, things he had to let go of because of what happened or qualities that would serve him moving forward."

"He wants to take in confidence and self-respect. He wants to feel solid and grounded."

"Great, help him invite in confidence and self-respect."

Leo nodded and closed his eyes.

After a few moments, I asked, "How is he doing now?"

"He feels lighter, like he can just do what he wants and not be so stressed about what anyone is thinking about him."

Integration

After Leo described how the exile was doing after inviting in these new qualities, I reinforced the importance of the next step in healing: *integration*. This step involves different ways to assimilate and sustain the changes that occur after an exile unburdens.

First, it's important to bring the protectors back in so they can see how the exile is doing now that it has been able to let go of its burden. I asked Leo to invite in the critical manager, the "keep busy" part, and various firefighters to check out the exile—the part who had been so anxious—so they could see how he was doing now.

"They like that he's at the dog park, happy, just a little kid who needs to play and not worry about stuff. He seems relaxed and they like that."

I let Leo know that the protectors would now be freed up to do different things they preferred to their usual roles.

"They like that. They're relaxing too."

In addition to bringing in the protectors to witness the exile's transformation, the exile needs the Self's support to integrate the changes and to trust that it's safe to exist without the burden. It's important for the Self to stay curious about what the part needs and to check on it regularly for at least a month or until the changes have been consolidated.

"That's great, Leo. It's going to be important for you to check on him every day, for at least the next month, so he knows you're really there and you can take care of him. Can you commit to doing that?"

Leo nodded. "I can make it part of my morning meditation."

He took a deep breath and let out a sigh. "I didn't realize how much feeling that part was holding. It's a big relief to let go of it."

Following Up

When Leo and I met a couple of weeks later, I asked him if he'd been able to stay connected to the young boy.

"Yes, I've been pretty good about checking in with him. Sometimes he still feels anxious, but it's different now because I just sit next to him. I don't push him aside and get busy. I get curious about why he's feeling anxious, and I remind him that I've got his back. Now that I have a sense of my parts, I understand that when I get an urge to drink or get super busy, it means a part of me is feeling anxious or disconnected and could use something from me."

This last step in the unburdening process, *following up*, is important to see how the newly unburdened part is doing. It ensures that the part is still in connection with the Self and hasn't taken back its burden. In the event that Leo's exile part had reverted back to his former way of thinking and feeling, this step would have helped to elucidate the reasons why and would have explored what the exile needed from Leo's Self to more fully unburden.

Appreciating the Protector's Dilemma

As you befriend your protectors, you'll come to appreciate the bind they are in. While the strategies they adopted to take care of you are often no longer useful or necessary, they don't trust that it's safe to let go of them. So while many parts of you may want stop vilifying certain foods, the part of you who polices your food (a manager) continues to feel urgently that your safety lies in eating the "right" food. It needs the Self to demonstrate that you will be okay whether you choose the salad or the cheesecake, that you can unburden the exiles who were made to feel shame or fear about their choices.

If you find that parts of you become frustrated with a target protector for persisting in its habitual role (e.g., a food-policing manager is desperate for a bingeing part to quit it), you may find it helpful to validate their frustration and then spend some time helping them consider the target protector's viewpoint and positive intentions. Context is important. A protector who has lived with scarcity, due to situations like poverty or parental burdens, may have a much harder time not focusing on having enough food than someone who has restricted in an environment where there was enough food and it was available at predictable times.

Protective parts also incur more risks if you belong, or have belonged at some point, to groups that are treated as inferior in the dominant culture. Choosing not to diet, for example, is riskier for someone who is female and riskier still for someone who is fat. Revealing your body and feeling neutral or even good about it can expose you to more harm. As Roxane Gay (2017) related, "I am never allowed to forget the realities of my body, how my body offends the sensibilities of others, how my body dares to take up too much space, and how I dare to be confident."

It is important to get curious about the ways in which the target protector has been working to keep you safe by getting you to look or seem a certain way or the ways it's tried to hide or compensate when that wasn't possible. Generally speaking, your protectors are as strong as the current conditions, internal and external, call for. The greater the exiles' pain, or the more numerous and oppressive the cultural burdens that come to bear on your system, the more extreme and committed to their tactics your protectors become. In addition, some protectors act to suppress or protect several exiles. When this is the case, unburdening one exile won't be enough to fully liberate the protector from its role. This was Leo's experience. While unburdening the anxious nine-year-old helped his protectors ease up considerably, he needed to unburden several more anxious exiles before his protectors completely shifted out of their roles.

This was also the case for Vanessa, whose extreme feelings about weight loss reflected the complex matrix of legacy burdens her protectors were dealing with. While the work we'd done thus far had helped her critical manager become more compassionate regarding her depression, it continued to be vehement about her need to lose weight.

I asked Vanessa if she was curious about her manager's steady focus on her weight and how it felt about its role. By asking these questions, I hoped to help Vanessa unblend a bit more from the part so she could get curious about its intentions and impact.

"That's kind of a tricky question. Parts of me think the reason I've been so successful is because this critical part has worked as hard as it does to help me look good."

I noted the alliance between the critical part and other parts of her system. "So other parts credit the critical manager for helping you be successful. Would you see if they would be willing to give some space so we can get to know more about this critical part who's so focused on weight?"

Vanessa sighed. "My weight has always been an issue for me, but not to the point where it was a real problem. But the number I saw on the scale this morning, *that* is a problem."

"That's what the critical part is saying?"

Vanessa nodded. I asked if she was interested in getting to know this part. When she said yes, I asked if she could see if the part would be willing to separate a little so Vanessa could hear more about its distress. It shared how frustrated it was with Vanessa for gaining weight and not doing the things it believed would get her back to her pre-baby weight.

"It's saying that this is a slippery slope, that I really need to pay attention."

I was curious about the protector's concern. "Do you know what it means by 'a slippery slope'?"

"Yes, in the past, it kept me in a pretty consistent routine—going to the gym before work three times a week and taking martial arts classes two nights a week. It kept things in check. But now I can barely get to the gym once a week. Things are just so hectic. I try to work out at home, and when it happens, that's great, but it's not happening as much as I'd like to. There's always something interrupting me. This part is not happy about it. Really, many parts of me aren't happy, except the part that likes having time with the kids."

Vanessa contemplated this a bit before adding, "I guess that's pretty important."

I agreed and asked her if she could see or sense the critical part as it focused on weight loss. "Do you notice the part as you're speaking about it?"

"I feel it in my arms, a tightness here and here," she responded while running her hands down both forearms.

"Would it be okay to stay with the tightness?" I asked.

After she nodded, I continued, asking, "Do you still feel curious about this part?"

"I don't feel very curious about it. Mostly I feel like this part is right. I feel like I will be taken much more seriously if I look more the part of a corporate executive. That's not going to happen at my current weight."

She continued, saying, "I'm a Black woman in a White–male dominated field. As much as parts of me hate it, the reality is that it's better for me if I'm thinner. Being pregnant and taking time off, I feel like I've already lost a lot of ground. I worry that I'm not as relevant as I was when I first started in this department, before I had kids."

Vanessa's protectors had good reason to be concerned about the intersecting impact of her gender, race, and weight on her advancement at work. Studies show that women are paid less than men and that this gap in earnings widens during child-rearing years (Kochhar, 2023). Women also get paid less as their weight increases (Roehling et al., 2018), and Black women, relative to White women, are more often passed up for promotion (McKinsey & Company, 2022). In fact, discrimination on the basis of weight is legal in all but two states and six cities in the United States (Yurkevich, 2023).

Vanessa closed her eyes once more and elaborated on her lack of curiosity. "Yeah, I guess you'd say I'm pretty blended with parts who like this critical manager—not for how harsh it can be but for how it keeps pushing me to do better."

"Where do you notice those parts, Vanessa?"

"More in my head, my thoughts," she replied.

"Let them know you hear them and ask them if they'd be willing to separate from you a little so you can get to know more about the critic and its focus on weight loss. Let them know we're not going to try to get rid of this part. We just want to learn more about what it's trying to do for you and which parts it's protecting."

With her eyes closed, Vanessa said, "They're okay with sitting off to the side, over here," gesturing with her hand to a spot two feet away.

"Okay, that's great. Thank them for that and remind them that they can come back in anytime they need our attention."

After a few seconds, Vanessa opened her eyes. "Okay, they've sat back."

"Great. Now see if you can find the part who focuses on losing weight. Is it still in your forearms?" I asked.

"Yes, it's the same tightness."

"How do you feel toward this part as you focus on it now, Vanessa?"

"I am so tired of this part. I know you're going to tell me that's also a part. I'll see if I can get it to give me some room."

"Great catch," I replied, acknowledging Vanessa's discernment of a part who disliked the critical manager.

Vanessa took a deep breath and said, "Okay, it's agreeing to give me some space."

"Thank it for that and now shift your focus back to the critical part. How do you feel toward it?"

"I feel open to hearing from it."

"Great. Let it know you're interested and also let it know that we will watch for other parts so they don't take over."

Vanessa nodded. "It says it's very concerned about me looking good. If it didn't keep pushing me to lose weight, I'd just accept my body the way it is, and that would be bad."

"Ask it to tell you why it would be bad."

"People won't take me seriously if I don't lose weight. If I can't take care of myself, then people aren't going to respect me professionally."

"Can you ask this part how it came to believe that gaining weight means you can't take care of yourself?"

Vanessa closed her eyes to focus on the part. "You mean aside from that's what practically everyone believes?"

I noticed within myself some frustrated parts who were poised to blend with me as Vanessa spoke to the reality that she would be judged by some people for the ways her body had changed. I reminded these parts that if they didn't take over, I could, from Self, remain clear about another reality: that if Vanessa's critic and other protectors allowed it, she could go to and heal the exiles that carried shame about her body. Once she did that, Vanessa would not be *as vulnerable* to external bias because parts of her wouldn't be as likely to absorb it in the same way. She'd also be more likely to get help for them when she noticed parts who were getting hurt.

I remained quiet to allow Vanessa to say more about what the critical part feared would happen if it relaxed its focus on her weight.

After a few moments, Vanessa continued, saying, "As I listen, what I'm hearing is that being thinner is better, that it gets me more respect from my male colleagues but also from the women I work with. Probably even more than the men, actually."

"See what the part wants to share about its experience with this, about being judged or less respected for what your body looks like, for how much you weigh."

Vanessa sighed impatiently and shook her head. "I'm noticing a voice that's saying, 'Here we go, we're going to analyze this when it's not something I can really do anything about, it's reality.'"

I asked Vanessa if the part who felt frustrated was the critical part who focused on weight loss or a different part.

After a brief pause, Vanessa responded, "It's a different part. I'm asking it to give me some room to check this out, even though it's really skeptical there's much value to doing this."

"Great," I replied. "Let it know you appreciate that. We just want to get to know more about how the critical part who focuses on weight loss came to feel the way she does."

Closing her eyes once more, Vanessa said, "I'm asking all the parts that are interrupting to give me some room so I can be curious about the critical part."

She paused for a while.

"What are you noticing now?" I asked.

"The part is reminding me how critical my father was when I gained weight. He has always been very concerned about his own appearance, and my mother's weight was always a problem for him."

"Can you ask the critical part if it would like to say more about what that was like?"

Vanessa nodded, then added, "This part hated how my father treated my mother—always putting her down for her size and talking about how beautiful she was when she was thinner."

I asked Vanessa if the critical part was stuck in a particular time or place in the past.

"It's telling me about the time when I came to stay with my father and stepmother after I'd been with my mother for most of the summer. I think I was maybe fourteen or fifteen. My mother dropped me off and I could see the disappointment on my father's face when he saw me. He made some comment about how he could tell I'd been enjoying my summer. He wasn't more explicit, but he didn't have to be. I saw the look on his face. I felt so much shame and also so much dread about being stuck there for the rest of the summer."

"How are you feeling toward this part as you hear this?"

"I feel bad for her."

"Let her know you feel bad for her and see what else she wants you to know."

"She's reminding me about how alone she felt, how awful it felt to have no choice about staying at my dad's. She didn't want to be there, she just wanted to be with her friends. He guilt-tripped her for that—told her she was selfish. Her stepmother was always trying to get her to join the family when she just wanted to be left alone. She didn't like my stepbrothers, and that upset her father. It wasn't convenient for them. *She* wasn't convenient for them."

"That sounds really hard. Let her know you feel for her, Vanessa. See what it's like for her to have your attention and compassion."

"She relaxes a little. It's a relief to speak for how alone and misunderstood she felt. And as hurt and mad as she felt, his opinion mattered to her. That comment about her body stuck with her."

"And it's still with her, isn't that right? She's committed to you not gaining weight and being shamed like your mother?"

Vanessa nodded. "That's why this is so hard for her. She's convinced everyone at work, especially my boss, has a different opinion of me now. I've had more than enough time to get back to my pre-pregnancy weight."

"How close are you to this part, Vanessa? Can you see her or sense her?"

Vanessa closed her eyes. "I can't see her, but I can sense her. There's less tightness in my arms, but I'm still tense all over, just not at ease, like she's on guard."

I said, "See how close you can get to her. Let her know you understand how hard she's been working to keep you from being shamed through her focus on managing your weight. Let her know you get how hard it is for her now when she can't get you to lose the weight you gained during your pregnancies."

Vanessa exhaled as she connected with the critical part. "The acknowledgment helps her relax a little."

"Ask her which parts she's protecting by trying to get you to lose weight."

"She wants me to be clear that the weight I'm at right now is something she never would have imagined. It's unacceptable in so many ways. She's getting more wound up as we're talking about it."

"I can see that. I'm wondering if you can ask the part how old she thinks you are."

Closing her eyes, Vanessa said, "Huh, that's interesting. She just looked up at me like she was seeing me for the first time. She thinks I'm her age, around twelve or thirteen."

"Let her know how old you are and see how she responds to that."

"It's a little hard for her to believe. She isn't sure exactly what that means, but that question got her attention. She's curious about me."

"Let her know that you're not a kid anymore. If she gives you a chance, you can show her that you can take care of her and the parts she's been trying to take care of by trying to get you to lose weight—the ones who carry so much fear and shame. Ask her if she'd like that."

Vanessa noticed a wave of exhaustion pass through her. While still skeptical that it was safe to stop focusing on weight loss, the critical manager registered its relief at the prospect of Vanessa's Self taking over.

I let Vanessa know that, if she was ready, she could help get that distressed and angry teenager out of where she was stuck in the past, at her father's house with no options and with so much scrutiny on her body. "We don't have a lot of time left, so let her know we will come back to help the exiles she's worked so hard to protect, the ones who were so hurt by her family's judgment and mocking. In the meantime, she doesn't need to stay stuck back there if she doesn't want to be, nor do the exiles. See if there's somewhere she'd like to be with you in the present."

Vanessa sighed. "She says she's open to trying that and seeing what happens."

"Great, ask her where she'd like to be. Let her know that it can be with you or somewhere she finds safe and comfortable, either real or imagined."

Vanessa was quiet for a moment. "She says she wants to curl up on the couch with a fuzzy blanket and sleep for a while. She's so tired."

"Of course she is. Let her know you'll check in on her. She can also let you know if she needs your help. And we can do the same with the exiles."

Over time, as Vanessa helped the exiles release their shame, the critical manager stopped berating her for not losing weight. It became more trusting as it observed Vanessa's Self-leadership at work, redirecting conversations about food and her body and continuing to support the parts who held concerns about how she was being evaluated by the largely White male leadership team. Vanessa's involvement in a group for women of color in cybersecurity further bolstered the critical part's confidence in her Self.

Protection Has Its Costs

Leo and Vanessa's protectors had been working so hard for so long that neither of them realized how much energy and effort went into their respective strategies. It was only after they got into a relationship with these parts that they understood the impact on their systems, how taxing it was to keep trying to exile vulnerability and guard against further harm.

While this is true for all of us to some extent, it's particularly the case for people whose bodies are treated as inferior by the dominant culture. Living with bias, internal or external, is corrosive. In the face of ongoing systemic oppression and the minimization or dismissal of its impact, some protectors will have a harder time seeing the upside of easing up on their efforts to guard against harm and will remain locked in chronic states of stress and disconnection. Leo and Vanessa's managers are good examples of the productive, self-reliant strategies that parts adopt to get by in the dominant culture.

When we blend with our protectors, we often fail to consider the impact that they have on our minds and bodies. Whether they're overriding or disconnecting us from our physical needs, or leading us to treat parts of ourselves or our bodies with contempt, we typically don't realize the toll that they take on us until a competing perspective, life event, or symptom grabs our attention.

My personal experience living with a physical disability has helped me appreciate the dedicated efforts of my protectors *and* the consequences of their continued efforts to spare me the pain of being judged in a culture that has such a hard time accepting differences. When I was seventeen, I suddenly lost the sight in my left eye after a year of laser surgeries for a condition that was likely related to my premature birth. My family was overwhelmed and didn't talk about this abrupt loss. My protectors dealt with the helplessness and shock I felt by dedicating themselves to getting on with my life, graduating from high school and going to college. A year or so after losing my sight, I developed a permanent cataract. The iris of my left eye was now covered by a greenish gray cloudiness that made my disability something I could no longer hide.

My cataract was visible for the next ten years, when I was finally able to get a prosthetic contact lens. Only then did I realize how hard parts of me had been working to shield me from being fully aware of how stressful it was to navigate others' reactions to my appearance. I didn't realize how physically and emotionally draining it had been to anticipate and be met by others' stares, comments, and questions, which ran the gamut from mildly irritating and intrusive (e.g., "Is that your real eye?") to invalidating and enraging (e.g., when a professor insisted that my cataract was a sign of my "adolescent need to be unique," having assumed incorrectly that I had the option to cover or remove the cataract).

Because I asserted myself in these instances by speaking for the parts who were outraged, I believed I'd handled things well. Several of my managers were skillful at suppressing a lot of the fear, grief, and self-consciousness that other parts of me felt. They found ways to minimize or disconnect from the reality of my vision loss and my altered appearance. Living in urban areas, for example, offered options for public transportation that helped me avoid the vulnerability I sometimes felt (and still feel) because I relied on others to drive. In addition, these protectors had me focus on how fortunate I was that I could still see out of one eye, that my eyes still moved in sync with each other.

As I've reflected on my experiences, I realize how different cultural burdens shaped my own and others' response to my vision loss. My family's "have strength" motto was an ancestral legacy burden that went back many generations, and it still echoes the dominant culture's emphasis on overcoming adversity. My aversion to considering myself as someone with a disability certainly stemmed from attitudes I absorbed from the larger culture regarding disabilities, that I was somehow less than, different, or defective. It manifested in my habit of referring to my non-sighted eye as my "bad" eye, something I no longer do. As I've continued to do this healing work, I've learned more about what supports my system. The reality is that my inability to see anything out of my left eye has resulted in difficulties with depth perception that make driving a significant risk and have led me to occasionally misjudge stairs so that I lose my balance or fall. Therefore, referring to my vision loss as an "impairment" minimized the reality of my daily lived experience. Referring to myself as "visually impaired" is also not inaccurate; I have vision in one eye and therefore am not considered legally blind. My use of the word *disability* feels right to me given I experienced a loss of the functionality I previously had. I'm aware that others might have other ways of describing their visual or physical differences.

I have great respect for the team of protectors that helped me negotiate the trauma of my vision loss and other painful events in my life. Their restriction, bingeing, criticism, overexercising, and preoccupation with "food as medicine" allowed me to soothe or ward off the terror, grief, anger, and shame that parts of me carried—feelings that might otherwise have immobilized me. These protectors helped me minimize what was happening and deny the extent to which I was considered different—and to some, off-putting—in a culture that is so focused on appearances. Their efforts were successful, but they also caused considerable suffering, as I had many exiles who were left alone for many years with their fear, sadness, and confusion about my appearance, which I was told would continue to change as I got older. As I continue to grapple with burdens related to ableism, I've identified parts of myself who feel grateful that my prosthetic lens gives me the option to reveal or keep my disability hidden and parts who feel guilty about having that choice while others do not.

I also have parts who question whether, if I were truly accepting of how my disability changed my appearance, I would want to wear a prosthetic lens at all. I've come to realize that, given what I know about my body and how it's received in this world, the answer is more complicated than simply accepting myself. The choices I make depend to a large extent on the context in which I find myself. If I am with friends, it's easier not to wear my lens. However, if I'm going out in public or meeting people who have not known me without my lens, my decision depends on how much energy I have to deal with the reactions that my cataract elicits.

As my experience illustrates, our parts continue to scan the environment for potential harm, making a protector's job hard to let go of. The protector isn't wrong to track the social environment for dangers. The challenge is to heal the exiles in our systems so our protectors can trust that they aren't alone and that there is a Self who can work *with* them to find ways to safely navigate a world that so often shames and rejects all but the most "perfect" bodies.

Making Space for Parts Who Hold Grief

Releasing burdens related to food and your body inevitably involves grieving the many losses that these burdens have caused. It can be very hard to bear the regrets related to the years you spent in punitive practices designed to help you fit in, as can the realization that parts of you were unable to appreciate what your body had to offer earlier in your life. This may be especially true if you have endured losses due to age, illness, or injury. Spending time with these parts and giving them room to have their feelings clears the way for a more attuned relationship with your body as it is now.

Chrissy King (2023) emphasizes the importance of allowing for this mourning while acknowledging the shame that parts of you may also feel for continuing to struggle with wanting to change your body: "We live in a patriarchal and oppressive system in which there is social capital assigned to meeting standards of beauty. So it is no wonder that we may find ourselves still wanting to lose weight or change ourselves in some way to meet said standards of beauty" (p. 215).

Healing Is Not Linear: The Importance of the 5 Ps

If you're like most people, you have *many* parts who have taken on lots of messages that influence the way you see your own and others' bodies, often without your awareness. Therefore, helping your parts let go of their burdens takes a lot of what IFS refers to as the 5 Ps: *patience, perspective, presence, persistence,* and *playfulness*. It takes time and effort to stay present to your internal dynamics so you can identify which parts of you still need healing, and it takes patience and persistence to keep showing your parts that you can take care of them as they take the risk to let go of their customary ways of thinking, feeling, and behaving. Finally, while you may find it hard to find anything lighthearted about this process, a playful attitude allows you to relate to your protectors without taking their narrative to heart. For example, as you notice a part saying something brutal about your appearance, you can greet it with something like "Whoa! What's going on? What's got you so riled up? What would you need from me right now to ease up?"

As you continue to do the work of liberating parts from their extreme roles and emotions, you become increasingly Self-led. However, because you have many burdens and the external environment continues to recruit your protectors, this process is inevitably a bumpy one. You will repeatedly get blended with parts who are either burdened or vulnerable to taking back their burdens. For this reason, it's helpful to have a practice that allows you to track what's happening inside so you can more quickly intervene from Self when this is happening.

In the following chapter, you'll learn how to support your parts through a Self-Led Eating and Well-Being practice. In addition to helping you continue to unburden, it will allow you to make decisions about food and your body that emanate from your core wisdom much more of the time.

Chapter 6

Developing a Self-Led Eating and Well-Being Practice

"It's actually very important what we do as individuals inside of the landscape of our own bodies. [. . .] What each of us practices at the scale of our individual lives is what is then possible for us at a large scale. [. . .] I'm a microcosm of all the possible liberation, justice, pleasure, and honesty in the universe and I act accordingly."

–adrienne maree brown

'd been meeting with Amanda for a couple of years when I referred her to a residential eating disorder treatment facility. The program helped her to start healing the traumas that gave rise to her eating disorder. However, like many of my clients, the most difficult chapter of her recovery was the transition from the structured environment of the program to the home she shared with her family.

In one of our initial sessions after she left the program, Amanda recounted how she had gone out to dinner with her friends. Feeling like she ate too much, she found herself doing what she would typically do in such a moment.

"I went outside to the alley to throw up," she said. "But then I remembered I could work with my parts."

Prior to treatment, Amanda had rarely been able to shift course once she got the impulse to purge. Now, however, not only was she able to pause, she was able to do so with compassion for the part who wanted to purge. She had a conversation with this part and helped it relax when it shared its distress about the part who got her to eat "so much." Then she went back inside the restaurant to join her friends and enjoyed the rest of the evening.

I often tell this story because it was the moment when I fully registered the power of the IFS model. It showed me how Amanda's relationship to her internal experience had been transformed. Despite the fact that her external environment was virtually the same as when she'd left a month prior, she was now far less vulnerable to the provocations that had led parts of her to become extreme in the past. While Amanda was able to do this work on her own in individual therapy, some people need intense family therapy so their family members aren't as activating to them.

I observed the same kind of change in Christina from chapter 4, who got a lot of comments from the members of her family for her size or for what she was eating. As she unburdened many of the "shoulds" that parts of her had been carrying, she found they didn't impact her in the same way. While she continued to feel intruded upon and angry when someone judged her, she didn't get flooded with shame as often, and she was less likely to question her sense of what she needed or wanted.

With less internal turmoil to distract her, Christina found it was easier to notice and respond to her parts, who naturally competed to get their needs met. For example, the part who wanted to relax and watch TV often bickered with the part who lobbied for her to cook dinner. Decisions like these became much easier to make when her parts were no longer yoked to beliefs about their inherent goodness, desirability, or longevity. Still, on days when life got stressful for one reason or another, and especially on days when she faced judgment from others about her size or food choices, Christina sometimes had a harder time staying Self-led.

Achieving and Maintaining Unburdened Eating via a Self-Led Eating and Well-Being Practice

When you have many parts who are burdened, you don't have a lot of access to your Self and its wisdom about what your system needs. Instead, as your protectors work to ward off the exiles' pain and prevent further wounding, they become increasingly polarized with each other. You can't see the sun for the cloud cover. When you don't eat enough food or what you really want, for example, because parts of you are restricting to lose weight, to be "healthy," or to compensate for what you ate the day before, other parts will grab whatever is available when your hunger or deprivation become intolerable. These parts will eat in a way that feels uncomfortable because they've eaten too quickly to alleviate the hunger, because they have to get what they can before the restricting part takes over again, or because they are desperate to escape the exiles' shame.

Unburdened Eating relates to the kind of relationship you can have with food and your body as you unburden the parts of yourself who hold extreme beliefs about food and your body to reconnect with your Self. The Self and your parts have an ongoing conversation that respects all the parts and their desires and needs, even if they cannot be met in a given moment. As you unburden, you'll find it easier to notice and respond to your parts because they will no longer be as saddled with shame and fear, as frantic, or as reactive to external rules or judgment.

That said, two things will make it difficult for you to stay connected to your core wisdom. First, even when your parts have taken the risk to let go of their burdens, they won't automatically trust your Self to lead the system—that trust develops over time as parts observe the Self *acting in real time* to take care of the parts of you who become extreme or more vulnerable. Second, you live in a culture where you are continually subjected to toxic messages about your body and pulls to take back or adopt new burdens (e.g., due to systemic oppression, aging, illness, developmental changes). A Self-Led Eating and Well-Being practice equips you with ways to notice when parts of you are getting extreme so you can find out why. Once you understand their reasons, you can help the parts resist reverting to their former (burdened) ways of being and feeling or help them unburden further.

The Components of a Self-Led Eating and Well-Being Practice

A Self-Led Eating and Well-Being practice is a compassionate process of regularly checking in with your parts and establishing predictable—though flexible—opportunities for meals and snacks (as well as rest, pleasure, movement, connection, spiritual practice, and so on) so parts of you don't get desperate. The importance of including a variety of psychological, somatic, and spiritual supports is important in distinguishing a Self-Led Eating and Well-Being practice from diet and wellness plans. While definitions of wellness vary, they tend to focus on physical health. Well-being, by contrast, "means much more than getting enough exercise or how we are feeling physically. It's about taking a holistic view and understanding how the dimensions of well-being—physical, emotional, social, clinical and financial—are intertwined and impact one another" (Muldoon, 2022).

With the access to Self-energy that unburdening allows, you will become clearer about all of the activities that support you. You can then negotiate with the different parts of yourself so that there's more balance and collaboration related to meeting these different wants and needs. When your choices don't align with your core wisdom, like when you eat beyond the point of what feels comfortable, don't get enough sleep, or start planning a diet, you treat these as important trailheads, signs that parts of you could use some attention or support. *This is what it means to lead from the Self.* You negotiate with the parts who have conflicting agendas about food and the body so there's more ease and kindness among them. You become clear about the importance of protecting yourself from further burdening by tracking threats to your Self-leadership from within and in the external environment.

It's important to acknowledge that your ability to unburden and stay Self-led will be much more difficult if you are actively struggling to make ends meet or bombarded by racist, patriarchal, anti-fat, and other oppressive cultural forces. When you don't have a lot of money or have to work multiple jobs, you may not be able to offer your parts the flexible and predictable options for the kind of food, movement, rest, and pleasure that support your well-being. What may be possible, however, is the most important aspect of a Self-Led Eating and Well-Being practice: the reconnection with your Self and its wisdom about what you have endured—and continue to endure—to stay in compassionate relationship with the different parts of yourself instead of being driven by shame and "shoulds" that have little relation to *your* lived experience. *You are the only one who knows what it's like to live in your body, in your current circumstances, and with your particular matrix of burdens.* As such, *you* are the expert of *your* system and *your* body. Rooted in this acknowledgment, a Self-Led Eating and Well-Being practice is also an invitation to get to know and heal the parts of yourself who make assumptions or judgments about parts inside of you and other people.

In this chapter, you'll learn about the different components of a Self-Led Eating and Well-Being practice that can help you when you get pulled off-center. These include:

- Discerning parts-driven from Self-led choices
- Developing Self-led intentions
- Cultivating a practice of Self-led oversight
- Engaging in a Self-led negotiation of your internal environment
- Nurturing a Self-led network
- Bringing your Self to heal external systems

These are not rules or principles but overlapping ways of helping you notice when you're relating to food or your body from a part rather than your Self. They will help you strengthen the relationship you have with your parts and facilitate their collaboration in the face of day-to-day stress and external pulls to find fault with or change your body.

Discerning Parts-Driven from Self-Led Choices

As you heal your burdened exiles and liberate the protectors who have worked hard to soothe their pain and prevent further wounding, you become increasingly embodied, meaning that you are more in touch with yourself and your body. This allows you to get clearer about the things that support you (e.g., food, rest, movement, social connection) and in what ways (e.g., how much, what kind, how often). Unlike the choices that emanate from burdened parts, Self-led decisions about food and your body are achievable and sustainable. That's because Self-led choices stem from the Self's consideration of what your internal family needs rather than the needs of a particular part.

For example, Christina related her surprise at realizing how much she disliked several of the foods she'd pushed herself to eat because parts of her believed they'd help her be healthy and lose weight. "I didn't realize how much I hate salad. I hate everything about it. I don't like many vegetables, and I hate all the work that goes into it. But I kept thinking, 'If I want to be healthy and lose weight, I need to eat salad.' And of course, other parts of me were like 'We don't care, we're not doing it.'"

Once Christina identified the two sides of the polarization—the health-minded and weight loss-focused parts who pushed the vegetable agenda and the parts who wanted nothing to do with it—she got curious about the positive intention of each.

The health- and weight-focused protectors carried legacy burdens related to illness among Christina's family members. Eating vegetables and other "healthy" foods protected parts who were saddled with fear about being blamed for getting sick.

For their part, the vegetable-hating parts recalled times when Christina was made to stay at the table until she ate her vegetables, often late into the evening.

Christina explained, "As a kid I wasn't allowed to get up from the table until I ate all of them. I spent many nights at the kitchen table by myself."

These power struggles reflected family legacy burdens around authority and obedience as well as weight and health.

Christina helped her health- and weight-focused protectors see that when they lobbied for her to eat more vegetables, they inevitably elicited pushback from the parts who hated eating them. As she helped them release their extreme beliefs about nutrition, weight, and health, these parts relaxed a bit.

For the first time, Christina was able to pay attention to the kinds of foods she found pleasurable *and* made her feel good. "I really like fruit, so I started having more of that. I realized I really enjoy smoothies with my breakfast, and every once in a while, I'll throw in a handful of spinach. I feel like I have more energy when I start my day this way, which could be related to a part who still feels virtuous when I have fruit and vegetables, but the important thing is that I don't stress about including vegetables and I no longer feel like there's something wrong—or will be wrong with me—for not liking them."

Christina's experience is a good example of how different options emerge when you unblend from protectors and their "good/bad" or "either/or" thinking. Instead of forcing herself to eat vegetables, Christina learned she could get a lot of the same nutrients by eating fruit or incorporating vegetables in foods she actually enjoyed. Her work with the part who was so focused on her health *and* the parts who felt controlled was what allowed this realization. She had become increasingly Self-led in her choices about food instead of being driven by parts. This aligns with the more recent suggestion made by Cece Sykes, an IFS lead trainer who specializes in the treatment of addictive processes—that "choice" be made the ninth "C" quality of Self (Sykes et al., 2023).

Recognizing when choices are parts-driven versus Self-led isn't always easy, especially when they're endorsed so highly by the outside world, as well as by other parts of the internal system.

For example, Leo often got positive feedback about being so productive. "People are always saying things like 'I can't believe you do all these great things, drawing and learning languages, and I can barely get off the couch.'"

In these moments, it was hard for Leo to see the downsides of being so productive. This changed when he tracked the sequences of his parts, which allowed him to see how his bursts of high activity were often followed by times when he couldn't motivate himself to do much of anything. He realized that when he privileged the "keep busy" part without considering the needs of his other parts, he was bound to keep experiencing this cycle of highs and lows.

While healing the exiles who motivated Leo's "keep busy" part was necessary to fully liberate this hardworking protector from its role, just getting some separation from the protector was helpful in shifting its behavior somewhat. With help from Leo's Self, the "keep busy" part observed that when it pushed less, other parts of Leo didn't crash in the way they had before. As Leo continued to relate to this protector from Self, it saw that Leo could unburden the exiles it had been warding off by staying so busy.

Developing Self-Led Intentions

Identifying agendas that come from parts (versus choices that come from Self) can help you stay present and attuned to the body you have *now*, not the one you had years ago or the one parts of you aspire to have in the future. That said, the demands of daily life can make it difficult to stay Self-led when it comes to eating and other self-care practices. For this reason, it can be helpful to have a sense, or overarching vision, of the activities and foods that support your well-being. As with all individual choices related to food and the body, Self-led intentions are flexible rather than static goals that privilege the needs of a few burdened or enthusiastic parts. They emerge as you survey all of your parts to see what each of them want and need.

To develop your own Self-led intentions, you may find it helpful to visualize a space to meet with the different parts of your system. You may envision or draw a table, cozy den, firepit, or place in nature—whatever works for you. Ask your parts to gather around so you can see or sense them in front of you. You'll find that polarized parts will typically situate themselves opposite each other, while parts who ally with one another will cluster together. Sykes and colleagues (2023) provide a number of exercises like this that you may find helpful to externalize and visualize your polarized parts in *Internal Family Systems Therapy for Addictions*.

As you welcome all of your parts, you can check in with them to get their input about which activities they find helpful and in what way (e.g., frequency, format, time of day, location). It's also important to consider factors such as your developmental stage, current stressors, and access to resources (e.g., time, energy, money, and support). As the leader of the system, the Self makes room for the parts' respective wishes and ultimately decides what's best for you in that moment.

Who's at Your Table?

As you focus inside, you'll likely notice various parts who hold different beliefs and feelings related to how you eat and relate to your body. See if you can get curious about the different roles these parts play in your system, especially the ones who hold big agendas (e.g., to lose weight, eat a certain way, get more muscular, be healthy, look attractive).

Ask the following questions. Don't think of the answers, just see what comes back to you from that place in your body.

- What beliefs or feelings do you hold?
- What led you to take on these beliefs/feelings/ways of coping?
- Do you protect other parts?
- What happens when you do what you do? Which parts do you polarize or align with?
- What or who in the outside world reinforces your feelings, beliefs, or actions?
- What would you need to let go of your feelings/beliefs or shift out of your role?

Some examples of parts of people I've known or worked with are listed in the following figure (pages 136–137). Remember that these labels only refer to the roles that these parts were forced into. See which of these resonate with you and, if it feels helpful, locate your own parts around a table as you see depicted in the figure. Please keep in mind that the names used are shorthand. While it's common for people to refer to their protectors by their primary protective strategy and exiles by the feelings and beliefs they're burdened with, it's important to remember that all parts have a range of thoughts, feelings, and ways of being. Also, parts will let you know what they want to be called, so it's important to ask them what they prefer.

Vanessa's experience illustrates how helpful it can be to identify and plan for activities that help you feel more grounded and connected to Self. For Vanessa, this was key to being able to shift out of the depression she experienced after several huge lifestyle changes in a relatively short period of time. "The hardest thing for me about having kids has been how little control I have—over how I feel physically, over my time and my space. When I was single, and even when Kevin and

I moved in together, things were so much simpler. Now I feel like I'm constantly juggling and dropping the ball. I've had to do a lot of work with my perfectionistic part because it leaves me with no time to take care of myself."

Vanessa's perfectionistic part, another manager who was a close cousin of the critic she'd done a lot of work to unburden, had a hard time relaxing its standards anywhere. Like the other managers with which it allied, this part continued to push for high levels of performance at work, with her parenting, and in her workouts.

Vanessa got more depressed as she kept making fitness goals for herself that she couldn't accomplish. "I would grid out my schedule, and it seemed reasonable to plan for three classes a week, but then I wouldn't even get to one class. I constantly felt like I was failing."

As she focused on her perfectionist's drive to get her back "on track," Vanessa realized this part would not accept that her life had changed. It held onto ideas about her body that didn't fit her current circumstances. When she asked the part to say more about its frustration, it replied, "I want the body I had when I was thirty. I was strong and I looked a lot better than I do now. Most days, I did something to move my body and it made me feel great. Now I can go a couple of weeks without doing anything."

Vanessa got curious about the perfectionistic part's agenda for trying to get her as fit as she'd been before she had kids. In response, the part listed several reasons why it felt fitness was so important: "It helped me relax, it got the stress out, I was stronger, it's good for my heart. I want to be able to do things with my kids. I'm an older mom."

While each of these points had some merit, the stress of feeling like a failure took a toll on Vanessa's mood and well-being. When the perfectionistic part pushed her to do three to four intense workouts a week, other parts, who felt exhausted by the perfectionist's demands, would respond by avoiding exercise altogether.

Who's at Your Table?

MANAGERS

"Critic"

Part who finds fault for various reasons: "What's wrong with me that I . . . let myself go, can't lose weight, can't get in shape, don't take better care of myself?" (Closely related to "Perfectionist.")

"Restrictor/Dieter"

Part who pushes for weight loss; tracks food and exercise, varying amounts of one to make up for, or feel deserving of, the other.

"Comparer" ("I'll have what she's having.")
"Competitor" ("No pain, no gain.")

Parts who override the body's needs to match or do more than others; focus on external metrics to prove worth.

"Time Traveler"

Part who holds an image of the body you had in the past or one it aspires to have in the future.

"Food Police"

Part who assigns moral value to foods (e.g., white foods, processed foods are "bad"). (Closely related to "Orthorexic" and "Meal Prepper" parts who hold extreme beliefs about health and wellness.)

"Perfectionist"

Part who works tirelessly to align with external standards regarding appearance and overall performance.

"Isolator"

Part who tries to take up less space, limits social contact, wears clothes designed to hide the body or minimize attention.

"Compensator"

Part who emphasizes other attributes (e.g., people-pleasing, humor) as a way to "make up for" perceived flaws.

FIREFIGHTERS

"Overeater/Binger"

Part who eats to soothe emotional or physical discomfort; amount eaten may or may not exceed physical needs or equate with clinical definitions of a binge.

"Grazer"

Part who eats throughout the day.

"Dissociator"

Part who disconnects from/blocks sensations from the body.

"Body Checker"

Part who grabs parts of body/looks in mirror/ gets on scale to evaluate or confirm size and appearance; may be a response to critical manager, exile, or dissociative firefighter.

"Self-Harmer"

Part who cuts/picks to distract from emotional distress.

"Can't Be Bothered"

Part who avoids thinking about food or exercise; may be responding to critical, perfectionistic, and dieting parts.

"Rationalizer/Minimizer"

Part who acts to cut off shame and fear arising from managers' (internal and external) judgments.

"Distractor"

Part who uses substances and other activities (e.g., exercise) to suppress feelings and/or hunger and fullness.

SELF

EXILES

Parts who feel deprived, worthless, ashamed, traumatized, scared, vigilant, rejected.

Vanessa explored what the perfectionistic part worried would happen if it allowed her to adopt a fitness plan that was less extreme and more feasible given the demands of her current life. It revealed that it protected parts who feared Vanessa would lose an important aspect of her identity as well as her connection with her husband amid all of the disruptions that came with motherhood and aging.

"Fitness was something we used to do together, and I worry about how not sharing that will affect us. I know my father was less attracted to my mother after she had kids. He spent less time doing things with her. Even though Kevin tells me this isn't an issue, a part of me has this fear. He's not going to the gym either, but he's always going for long runs and lifting weights. Not the kinds of things I want to do or have time for."

While Vanessa realized that her intense focus on fitness compensated for the uncertainty that other parts felt about her performance at work and as a parent, she hadn't realized how the perfectionistic part, like the critical manager, protected a young exile who feared that she, like her mother, would be abandoned if Vanessa wasn't as fit or thin as she had been. Before it could unburden, the young exile needed to be updated. She needed to see that Vanessa was an adult who could take care of and treat herself well—independent of Kevin's assessment of her. The exile felt relieved as Vanessa walked her through the home she shared with Kevin and their daughters. It helped the exile realize how different Vanessa's marriage was from that of her parents.

With more access to the Self-energy that this unburdening afforded, Vanessa got curious about what felt right to her given her current physical and emotional needs and time constraints. She realized that her main problem was getting to the gym. The time it took to arrange childcare and drive there made it impossible to go more than once a week. She needed something that was more convenient.

What ended up working for Vanessa was an online fitness program that offered a variety of workouts she could attend live or whenever she had time in her schedule. The program also connected her with an online community.

"We check in with each other and cheer each other on. I didn't realize how much I missed that part of going to the gym. It really motivates me, especially right now when I can't get out as much."

Unburdening the perfectionistic part and the exiles it protected also allowed Vanessa to see how many parts of her needed gentler, slower activities that the perfectionistic part previously would have regarded as "not counting" (e.g., meditation, restorative yoga). Including these kinds of activities in her schedule helped her feel more nurtured and less stressed. They also helped her stay more connected to her husband than she had been able to when she felt chronically depleted.

Connecting with Legacy Heirlooms

While in a waiting room at a doctor's office several years ago, I overheard a conversation between two sisters, both in their late seventies. One woman related that she was making chicken livers for dinner. "I have to get some chicken fat and some onions."

Her sister responded, "Chicken fat is bad for you."

This prompted the first woman to say, "Nana used chicken fat and it was delicious."

Without missing a beat, the second sister quipped, "And look what happened to her."

To my delight, the first woman turned to her sister and said, "Nana did a lot of good living and lived long enough."

They both laughed.

This made me think of my beloved Italian grandmother and all the times I watched her prepare a meal with care, from Sunday dinners to more mundane weekday fare. I helped stir the tomato sauce that, try as I might, I could never fully replicate in my own kitchen. I'd watch as she used a paring knife to peel the peaches she had for dessert, deftly removing the peel in almost one piece, often dipping the peaches into her wine. As I got older, my relationship with foods like lasagna, pasta, and bread became freighted with concerns about weight and health. It took some time for me to unburden so I could reconnect with the joy and connection I felt when I ate these foods.

I am grateful to my grandmother for passing on to me her love for food and cooking that helps me feel rooted even in the toughest of times. I carry within me the knowledge of how these skills and rituals helped her and my family survive the Great Depression. These Sunday dinners with my grandmother and the lessons they imparted have been, for me, a respite from my own, less extreme, trials and tribulations. They are an example of what IFS calls a *legacy heirloom*, a resource handed down across generations. Legacy heirlooms are values, messages, or traditions that connect you with your ancestral lineage and support your well-being. If you weren't taught to cook, you may have grown up with foods or rituals around food and family that you find grounding. If you didn't, because you grew up with a lot of instability or poverty, you may find it helpful to establish some traditions for the parts who missed out on these kinds of opportunities (to whatever extent is feasible given your current resources). As a friend of mine said, "For those of us who didn't learn to cook, we can always find a Jewish deli."

Cultivating a Practice of Self-Led Oversight: The Power of the Pause

Once you've developed a set of Self-led intentions, it helps to periodically pause to get a sense of what is and isn't working to support you. With so many external and internal "shoulds" and "shouldn'ts," it's easy for parts of you to have sidebar conversations outside of your awareness (i.e., unconsciously). Taking a moment to check in is extremely helpful in determining when this is happening.

If you're accustomed to blending with a manager who's concerned about getting it "right" or achieving certain goals, Self-led oversight, by comparison, will feel different. It involves a spacious, nonjudgmental survey of how you're doing rather than an evaluation of how "good" or "bad" you've been. Self-led oversight recognizes that the choices you make one moment may not feel right the next. Or that the next best choice for you may be unclear. For example, is the tightness you feel as you start to exercise something that will shift as you move, or is it coming from a part who's trying to tell you that it needs a different type of movement or some rest? Sometimes you might not know for a while. Self-led oversight helps you respond to your shifting needs and preferences in *real* time as well as *over* time. Similar to a mindfulness practice, Self-led oversight involves not only tracking the different parts of your system but intervening from the Self when parts of you are getting activated or overridden by other parts. Tom's experience provides a good example of this practice.

Tom was a thirty-four-year-old man who described himself as fat. He initially included exercise in his list of Self-led intentions because he felt better when he engaged in some kind of movement a few days a week. That said, of the activities he identified as most supportive of his well-being, movement was the one he found most challenging. It made parts of him more cognizant of the size of his body, and it often activated parts who felt uncoordinated and scared due to some early experiences with bullying. Growing up, Tom was frequently excluded by his classmates, who poked fun at his larger size and always chose him last for school sports teams.

To make it easier for the parts who disliked exercise, Tom put effort into exploring what kind of movement would be enjoyable for them and not make them feel too self-conscious. He found a weight-neutral yoga class that emphasized individualized attention, which these parts really liked. After a while, however, Tom started finding all kinds of reasons to avoid going. He noticed a critical part who started berating him for skipping class.

Since Tom had befriended this critical part of himself, he was able to unblend from it fairly quickly to get curious about what was causing him to avoid class. He discovered that other parts of him had feelings about being the only man in the class and not doing something more "masculine." He also noticed parts who were uncomfortable with the new teacher, a woman who wasn't as skillful at offering modifications that would help him enjoy the class and get as much out of it. His "avoidant" parts had been trying to protect him by not going to class. With this realization, Tom put his energy into finding a different teacher instead of finding fault with himself.

Tom's relationship with his wife, Alyssa, provided another opportunity for Self-led oversight that made him realize he needed to make some changes. Alyssa had cut out all refined sugar and flour from her diet because she believed they were addictive. In the past, Alyssa's restriction and disdain fed Tom's exiles' shame as other parts of him criticized him for not being able to match her self-discipline. As he attended to his parts, he realized his problem was not a lack of discipline. While he respected Alyssa's wish to avoid foods that activated her so much, he asserted that it was not his responsibility to make sure she wasn't ever around these foods. Together, they decided it would work best if they kept the food that Alyssa found challenging in a separate cabinet.

When Tom checked in to see how his parts felt about this arrangement, they gave him the thumbs-up, so when he noticed a few weeks later that a part of him was "sneaking" food to eat when Alyssa wasn't around, he got curious. "I asked the part who was sneaking food what was going on, why it was hiding stuff, and what it worried would happen if I ate these foods out in the open. The part reminded me of a couple of times recently when it sensed Alyssa's contempt. She didn't say a word, but this part could feel it."

Tom realized he had some more work to do to fully heal the young exile who was stuck in the past with classmates who bullied him about his "man-boobs" and for what he was eating. He let Alyssa know about the parts who felt hurt, a young exile and the protector who was sneaking food to avoid her judgment. Alyssa admitted a part of her *had* been feeling contemptuous of Tom for "not doing anything" about his weight. Fortunately, because Tom had previously shared how painful it was to have his food and body policed by the adults he grew up with (e.g., his parents, grandparents, teachers, coaches, random strangers), Alyssa quickly apologized and committed to doing more work with the part who was leaking contempt, making it more possible for her to learn more about the parts of her that the contempt was trying to protect. Tom's parts' trust in his Self grew with this important interaction.

In addition to checking in with your internal system, the Self oversees your external environment. Self-led oversight of your food environment is especially important as you're healing burdens related to food and the body. Generally speaking, when you have the resources (e.g., money, time, energy), the Self acts like a good parent and provides meals and snacks—at predictable times and in response to shifting needs—that are pleasurable to *and* support the well-being of the different parts of your system. In this way, Self-Led Eating and Well-Being aligns with certain aspects of the Division of Responsibility in Feeding model (Satter, 1986), Intuitive Eating (Tribole & Resch, 2020), and "food caretaking" (Kinavey & Sturtevant, 2022).

Keeping in mind that *within you is a Self who knows what you want and need*, if you have many burdened parts (i.e., less access to Self-energy), you may find it helpful to work with a therapist or dietitian who can help you discern the kind of food environment that facilitates your healing. With their guidance and your continued checking in with what does and doesn't work for your system, your confidence in your own ability to know what your parts want and need—and to give it to them—will grow.

Most clients with eating issues have concerns related to control, which emanate from their polarized protectors who have been duking it out for years, or even decades. Managers want to regain control over the firefighters, and firefighters long to wrest free of the managers' tight grip and harsh commentary. Approaches that advocate for unconditional permission to eat can be simultaneously exciting and terrifying. While your firefighters (as well as some exhausted managers and deprived exiles) will be relieved by the prospect of having unconditional permission to eat, other parts (e.g., managers who still believe you need to lose weight and don't trust your firefighters to not take over, exiles who have been shamed for wanting or having "too much") will find this suggestion frightening and overwhelming. Unconditional permission to eat what you want thus has the *potential* to heighten tensions between your polarized parts, who don't yet trust each other or your Self to mediate between them.

Suggestions to rely on hunger and fullness cues to guide your eating can be similarly activating to burdened protectors for two reasons. For starters, managers who rigidly cling to this recommendation can reinforce other parts' burdens of guilt and shame related to eating for pleasure, for self-soothing, or for distraction. Also, to the extent that parts can distort sensations of hunger and fullness to communicate their emotional needs, relying on these physiological cues can be misleading. For example, some parts can make you feel full. Others will default to hunger, as you saw with Mara in chapter 2, when she described her experience with Intuitive Eating and how she always felt a bit hungry, which frequently led her to eat something. This made her more fearful of her appetite. Mara would learn that her hunger was often related to both physiological deprivation and her lonely and shame-filled exiles. She also found that many of her hunger cues were actually parts' reactions to the diet-minded manager who lurked behind the parts of Mara who wanted to eat intuitively, urging them to eat less.

As you unburden and become more Self-led, you'll become more adept at discerning what your parts need in the current moment. You'll find it easier to distinguish emotional needs from physiological needs. More important, you won't be as concerned when you eat for emotional reasons, because you will know this is not the catastrophe that burdened parts make it out to be. While cookies might not be the most effective way to cope when a part of you really needs a nap, some attention, or a hug from your Self and a good cry, it isn't the worst thing, and it actually might help a little in the moment. In that case, it is especially important to notice and gently hold back the parts who find cookie eating problematic—this way, they won't pummel you or the part who ate what it wanted.

Depending on the burdens that parts of you still carry, it may be helpful to keep certain foods out of the house and to enjoy them in external settings. It may also be helpful to keep these foods inside the house but in certain areas or in amounts that are large enough to satisfy the needs of parts who carry burdens of scarcity *and* moderate enough to reassure the parts who fear losing control. Of course, this is a very difficult balance, and what's most important is that there's a Self (your own or that of someone you trust) who can respond with compassion and curiosity when various parts who still carry burdens take over the system and upset the parts with whom they're polarized.

It's important to keep in mind that these suggestions about curating your food environment are *suggestions*. They are based on my experience working with many people who get excited and scared when they are not in a regimen (i.e., dieting or trying to change their bodies), which causes them to revert back to the comfort of rules and structure because their protectors keep taking over. They're designed to support *you* as you continue to unburden the parts who carry fear or shame about, or who polarize in relationship to, certain foods (or types of movement, and so on). As with all suggestions related to food and the body, what's most important is that *it's your body*. Ask *your* parts what feels right and notice the different reactions. You may find that unconditional permission to eat is exactly what your system needs, especially if you have parts who have known years of too many rules and restrictions. Or you may notice that while it initially feels right, parts of you find it more challenging over time or in certain contexts. The important point is to keep asking your parts what they need and to extend loving care to those parts who continue to worry about what other people think you should be doing with your food or your body.

If you choose to organize your food environment while you develop more trusting relationships with and between your protectors, it will be important to let your parts know that you understand why it might feel bad to some of them to not have access to these foods in the way they would like. If these parts object (e.g., "Why can't I just eat intuitively?" or "We hate being deprived!"), it's helpful to remind them that this decision is not the directive of a manager who is restricting or complying with external authority. Rather, it's a choice rooted in the Self's clarity about the need for more healing—the unburdening of exiles and trust-building with polarized protectors who are accustomed to either restricting or bingeing, to either being "good/healthy" or "bad/ eating whatever." This kind of compassionate acknowledgment of the parts by the Self is also helpful if you have a medical condition for which limiting or abstaining from certain foods or types of movement is recommended. Gradually, as you do this work, it will be easier to stay Self-led with these foods around.

Mara's experience well-illustrates the positive impact of Self-to-part negotiations of the food environment. She was someone who had spent most of her adult life vilifying foods high in fat and sugar, believing she was "one of those people who just can't eat those kinds of foods in moderation." While she felt hopeless about ever being able to have these foods "like a sane person would," restricting herself from eating them required a vigilance that other parts of her found exhausting and depressing.

Wanting to shift out of these painful extremes, Mara's Self extended a compromise: While parts of her still felt so unsafe with these foods, she would refrain from keeping large quantities of them in the house. She would, however, give the parts who hated being deprived access to these foods by buying them in smaller quantities or having them outside the house. By giving herself access to these foods, albeit in a structured way, Mara hoped to address the scarcity, shame, and fear that had activated her polarized protectors for so long.

Over the next few weeks, Mara experimented with eating breakfast and lunch at work, including some of the foods she typically restricted. While eating more during the day initially felt uncomfortable to some parts (e.g., those who compared her to dieting coworkers and believed she didn't need so much food during the day when she "wasn't doing anything"), it was relieving to others, as she noticed she had more energy and was able to concentrate better, especially later in the day. Most importantly, she discovered that she felt much less of a need to eat on the way home from work.

One night, feeling more confident in her ability to handle herself with foods she formerly restricted, Mara bought a jar of chocolate hazelnut spread along with her other groceries for dinner. She told herself she would eat a small amount but proceeded to go through most of the jar while watching TV late at night. A critical manager blasted her as soon as she woke up the next morning. "See, I told you! We just can't have this stuff around." Her diet-minded part got busy searching online for a new plan that would help her feel better fast.

This moment was painfully familiar. What was different this time was Mara's response. Instead of staying blended and spiraling into another day of bingeing or exercising and not eating until dinnertime, she took some deep breaths so she could get perspective (i.e., access some Self-energy). She comforted the parts who were upset and got curious about which part had led her to eat to the point of feeling sick and why.

As she paused to reflect, Mara realized that the firefighter who grabbed the chocolate resented the compromise of keeping certain foods out of the house. In addition, another part judged Mara's need to be so structured when it came to food: "If you were really making progress, you'd be able to have the chocolate spread at home and eat a little at a time."

This judgmental part activated Mara's exiles, who were still burdened with shame about wanting "so much" and being "out of control." The firefighter who bargained, "It's okay, I'll only eat a little" was met by a vigilant manager who carefully measured out two tablespoons of the chocolate hazelnut spread. This portion control activated an exile who was still stuck in the past with a mother who counted out Mara's animal crackers and kept an eye on how much chocolate milk she drank. This activated Mara's bingeing firefighter, who acted to soothe the exile's deprivation and block out its shame by eating the rest of the chocolate.

Tracking the sequence of parts helped Mara realize her mistake: She hadn't paused the firefighter who grabbed the chocolate in order to get curious about why it was doing this and to explore how other parts felt about bringing a larger quantity of a challenging food into the house. She acknowledged the positive intention of the parts who wanted to eat more freely *and* acknowledged the other parts who weren't ready for this. Mara's Self-led apology helped her parts feel validated and also more hopeful because they believed she appreciated their different perspectives and because they trusted her commitment to intervening more quickly in the future.

Engaging in Self-Led Negotiation of Your Internal Environment

It's extremely rare for all of your parts to align in terms of what they want or need at any given time, even when burdens aren't driving your decisions about the different things that support your well-being. There's a part who wishes you got the tacos instead of the fajitas, or the part who would have preferred a walk to the bike ride that other parts thought was great. While parts of you feel better when you make the time to plan for satisfying meals and snacks, other parts who hate meal prep would rather spend that time scrolling online. With decisions that are more complex—due to time constraints, demands from people around you, or potential consequences associated with certain choices—tension between the parts of you who want or need different things can become extreme. Focusing on one part won't get you very far, which is why Self-led negotiation is so important.

Self-led negotiation is akin to calling an internal team meeting to attend to the various parts' wants and needs. Sometimes the meeting is brief (e.g., when a need clearly supersedes a want), and at other times it will take more time (e.g., when equally compelling needs or wants compete for your attention). Sometimes you can carefully consider the pros and cons of a decision, while other times you have to act quickly, like a triage nurse in a busy emergency room, to figure out who needs your attention most.

Self-led negotiation borrows from some studies showing that people are more likely to act collaboratively, tolerate short-term delays of gratification, and persist in difficult tasks when they experience prosocial feelings such as gratitude, compassion, and pride (e.g., Dickens & DeSteno, 2016). Self-led negotiation aims to cultivate a "we're on the same team" sense of pride between parts who lobby for different options by helping them to: (1) appreciate each other's intended contribution to the system and (2) extend gratitude to the parts who agree to wait their turn in order for the system to meet a more pressing want or need.

Natalie's experience with physical therapy is a good example of this process. As someone who had always been active and able to accomplish the things she'd wanted to do physically, she had parts who had a hard time accepting that, at sixty-three, certain kinds of exercise were more challenging or off-limits. These parts believed that if only Natalie took better care of herself, she wouldn't be in so much pain. They were the ones who minimized the discomfort she felt in her knee until she could no longer walk down the stairs.

When Natalie started physical therapy, she noticed several parts who had something to say. One part believed it was a waste of time, that she would get better results "walking it out" every morning. Another part hated the exercises for how boring and uncomfortable they were and also because they frequently made her more aware of her limitations. A third part, who was anxious about how much pain Natalie was in and how much her knee problem might affect her functioning in the future, was eager to get to the sessions.

When Natalie checked in with her Self, she was clear that she needed physical therapy. However, since many of her parts didn't want to do it, setting a Self-led intention required a lot of negotiating. First, Natalie gathered her parts together and let the ones who didn't want to do physical therapy have some time to complain. She let them know she understood why they didn't want to do the exercises and then asked if there was something that would make it easier for them to comply with the therapist's recommendations. As she listened to these parts, she heard that they would have an easier time with physical therapy if it was no more than twice a week and if she scheduled something enjoyable after the appointments.

With her assurance that she would make good on these conditions, Natalie got the green light from the resistant parts to continue the course of treatment. While she followed through on her intention to attend the appointments, she noticed that she often failed to do the "homework" the therapist prescribed. In the past, she would have blended with a part who would have guilted her for not doing the exercises (e.g., "It's a privilege to be able to go to physical therapy and you're wasting it"). Now, however, she got curious about that part, as well as the parts it activated: a young exile who took on the guilt, an adolescent part who was pissed at being guilted, and yet another part who felt exhausted by the whole situation and didn't want to think about it anymore.

Natalie recognized the need to reconnect with her parts as a group to see what they needed to get along better. "First, I focused on the part who was being critical of me for not doing the exercises. I asked it why it was guilting me, and it said it does feel like physical therapy is a privilege. But mostly, it was afraid that I would never do the exercises and this whole thing would be a waste of time. When I let the critical part know this made sense, it pointed to another part who is really upset about how much pain I'm in. I hadn't realized the critic was trying to take care of this part."

Natalie continued, saying, "The critical part and the part who was upset were both sitting on one side of the table. On the other side were the parts who were avoiding the exercises. One part said the exercises are too painful. It couldn't even tell if the exercises were helping. Other parts said they felt like all of this was just too much work, that it was hard enough to get to the appointments."

As Natalie validated each of her parts, she noticed feeling calmer. She reassured them that she wouldn't favor one side over the others, that she knew each had a legitimate perspective: Physical therapy was necessary *and* it was also painful and a lot of work. As Natalie got curious with the parts about what would help, the ones who got her to avoid the exercises let her know that they needed her to say something about the pain to the therapist. This hadn't occurred to Natalie because she was so frequently blended with the part who minimized physical and emotional discomfort. The part who guilted her said it needed her to work with the parts who said, "We'll do it tomorrow" so she didn't keep blending with them and not doing the exercises. Finally, the parts who were exhausted needed to be appreciated for putting in the time and energy to do the exercises when there were so many other things they'd rather do.

By meeting with her parts as a group, Natalie helped them get a sense of each other's positive intentions and their needs. As they watched Natalie regard each part with compassion and gratitude, the parts became more tolerant of one another. Also, because Natalie attended to all of her parts, not just those whose agendas prevailed in a given moment, they had an easier time when they didn't get their way. They felt her compassion and they trusted they'd get their turn at some point.

Natalie described how this played out internally. "When parts of me don't want to get off the couch to do my exercises, I have a conversation with them. I say something like 'I get how much you'd rather not do this' or 'I get how nice it would be to stay in bed for a little while longer.' I remind them that I can do the modified versions of the exercises and that I'll stop if anyone is too tired or uncomfortable. When these parts agree to relax back so I can do the exercises, I extend gratitude to them for being willing. And I ask the parts who want me to do the exercises if they can extend some appreciation to the other parts—to the ones who don't want to do physical therapy—for being willing to step aside so this can happen."

On days when the exercise-hating parts wouldn't budge, Natalie had a similar interaction with the anxious parts who worried about her knee. "I acknowledge the anxious parts' concerns and let them know I appreciate them for allowing the other parts a day off. I remind them that I know the physical therapy is important, but this is for the long haul, and it won't work to force other parts to do what they don't feel up to that day. I reassure them that I will continue to work with the parts who dislike the exercises to see what they need moving forward. I've found that it really makes a difference when the parts who need a day off are grateful to the anxious parts for their willingness to allow that to happen."

As Natalie's knee improved, the inner negotiation regarding the exercises became more fraught because the motivation that came from being unable to walk had abated. All of her parts, with the exception of a part who held some concerns about her future mobility, were joined in their view that the exercises were boring and took up time they'd rather be putting to other interests. In this case, Natalie's Self needed to come in like a good parent would and assert the need to continue the exercises so she could maintain her knee strength. However, she continued to engage her parts with curiosity about how much and how often they were willing to do physical therapy. Natalie found that regularly taking a moment to express the pride she felt about their collaboration went a long way in securing their willingness.

Nurturing a Self-Led Network

Bias is contagious but so is Self-energy. Protectors often need to observe or connect with other people who have more Self-led relationships with food and their bodies before the protectors become willing to risk letting go of their habitual strategies of dieting or disconnecting you from your body. When they do ease up on these strategies so your exiles are exposed, they can feel scared and be tempted to revert back to old ways—what IFS calls *backlash*. Curating a network of people—friends, doctors, therapists, dietitians, mentors—who don't engage in anti-fat practices or rhetoric can help you recharge your Self-led intentions and make you less vulnerable to parts taking back their burdens.

This was true for Christina, who described how helpful it was to participate in an online support group as she continued her work to heal the intrepid manager in her system who periodically scared her about how her weight might be affecting her health. "Every so often, I hear that voice out of the blue, urging me to do something about my weight. It's been a habit for so long, and when I'm feeling vulnerable for some reason, like when I'm not getting along with my mother or when someone comments about my appearance, it starts getting on me for not being more careful."

Christina continued, saying, "This part says I'd feel and look better if I lost weight. It can still have a lot of power in my system, even though I've worked hard to unburden it and it's eased up a lot. It reminds me how much easier it was to find clothes I felt comfortable in when I was thinner, how much easier it was to move. I try to be patient and let this part know I understand why it misses my old body and why it believes I would get relief from losing weight. And parts of me *have* felt relief when I've lost weight, but not for very long. Instead, other parts of me feel traumatized from years of dieting and 'failing,' or not dieting and hating myself. They just won't go back to that. And that's really hard for this part of me."

While this manager's longing to lose weight hadn't shifted as much as parts of Christina would like, Christina's relationship with it had changed quite a bit.

"When this part takes over, I know something is off. I'm depleted, lonely, or anxious about something. I don't let it take hold of me nearly as often anymore. I let it know I understand that it's trying to help me and remind it that I can take care of my body better if I'm not putting myself through the wringer."

In these moments, Christina emphasized that supportive relationships were key to helping her stay grounded and Self-led. "What really helps this part is connecting with people who are doing their own work to unburden, people who don't want to spend the rest of their lives worrying about what they look like. I wouldn't be able to do this work if I didn't have them to support and inspire me."

Connecting with like-minded people helped Christina unblend so she could keep coming back to her own wisdom instead of getting pulled off-center by the latest scientific study on weight loss or someone else's unchecked bias related to health.

It helped her stay grounded when she received consultation for her slightly elevated A1C reading and the doctor recommended a protein and vegetable, very low-carb diet, including sugarless gelatin, sugarless hard candy, and no other sweets. "It was like handing me a loaded gun and then blaming me for shooting myself. It was 100 percent not going to work for me and then it would be my fault when it didn't." Christina's friend eventually recommended another physician whose approach was more respectful and attuned.

Christina related feeling proud of the work she did to unburden enough of the shame and fear that parts of her carried. She now felt entitled and able to advocate for herself. She was also aware of how her access to good health care in a metropolitan area allowed her the option to find another physician who could better meet her needs. If you aren't as fortunate to have this kind of access to weight-neutral providers, or if you could use some help in advocating for yourself in medical and therapeutic settings, you may find it helpful to check out some of the resources listed on https://haeshealthsheets.com/resources.

Christina's experience is a good example of the power of community in supporting your parts as they take the risks involved in letting go of their burdens. This healing goes both ways. Every time you trust your own wisdom instead of overriding it to comply with external rules and expectations, you contribute to the pool of Self-energy that's available to help others heal, which brings us to the sixth and final component of a Self-Led Eating and Well-Being practice: bringing your Self to heal external systems.

Bringing Your Self to Heal External Systems

When you become more Self-led, you naturally become interested in bringing your Self to heal the burdens in other systems, one of the four missions of IFS. For example, as you heal the burdens that parts of you have been made to carry about your own body, you may discover that you notice—and care more about—the different ways the dominant culture marginalizes other bodies. You may see with new eyes the harm that comes to those bodies that don't align with what the dominant culture prizes or deems acceptable. With more access to your Self-energy, you may appreciate the role you have played in perpetuating these unjust attitudes and practices, and you can find new courage to disrupt biased beliefs related to race, weight, health, ability, sexuality, and gender.

As we will explore in the next chapter, as you become more aware of how you treat your body and how deeply ingrained your judgments of others' bodies are, you will be more apt to notice the aggression and shaming attitudes you might have otherwise passed off as humorous, "factual," or concern for others. You might find yourself more likely to speak up or, at the very least, not engage when friends, family, and colleagues persist in harmful or unjust behavior or attitudes. You will likely become more motivated to heal the parts of yourself who are still vulnerable to diets or modifying your body to make it more acceptable. You will also be more likely to consider how your individual decisions regarding intentional weight loss factor into larger systems of oppression.

If you notice parts who feel some shame and guilt because other parts of you still long to lose weight or change your body via dieting, exercise, surgery, or weight-loss drugs, see if you can extend some compassion to both sides of this polarization. Caleb Luna (2023) emphasizes the importance of not hiding or shaming the parts of yourself who are still burdened: "If we don't externalize it and process it in supportive ways, then it can manifest in harmful ways [. . .] There can be anxiety that if we admit any of that nuance or complexity around fat embodiment, that all of our other work can be undermined or dismissed or leveraged against us when actually it's just like we're all complex humans doing our best and these are real day-to-day things."

These words reflect the essence of the IFS model and Unburdened Eating. The more compassion and curiosity you can bring to your conflicting parts, the more healing that will be possible for you, and ultimately, for others around you. Bringing your Self-energy to heal external systems, the sixth component of Self-led eating, is important because it helps you remember that healing is ultimately a collective enterprise. This awareness can inspire you to keep doing the work to unblend from and unburden the parts who are getting pulled to participate in oppressive systems dressed up as individual lifestyle or self-improvement plans.

By bringing Self-energy into all the areas of your life—family, work, friends—you can make the world a little kinder, less burdened, and ideally more accepting. This individual transformation can lead to actions that will disrupt the burdens at the institutional level. As Maya Angelou (2014) said, "Develop enough courage so that you can stand up for yourself and then stand up for someone else" (p. 68). In the next chapter, I'll go into further detail on how to bring your Self to heal external systems.

Chapter 7

Bringing Self-Leadership to Heal External Systems

"There's no safe haven of hating your body that doesn't
also rely on logic that marginalizes mine. If you hate the fat
on your body, that will color your perception of mine. Like
any virus, you do not get to decide that you are resistant.
You do not get to decide whether it is communicable.
Do not transmit the virus back to your fat friend."

—Aubrey Gordon

met Nia at a mindful eating workshop we both attended. We'd been invited to find a partner with whom we could spend the generous two-hour lunch break. Our assignment was to be conscious of the choices we made regarding what to eat and what to do during this time. As we made our way across the crowded hotel lobby, Nia shared her frustration about the assignment and the workshop more generally.

"It is difficult to sit in these rooms with all these people who don't have the first clue about what it's really like to be fat. I don't want to minimize what they're feeling, but you just can't compare what it's like for them with what it's like for me. And I'm looking at the presenter, who seems nice and like she knows a lot, but it's obvious she doesn't really know what it's like to be fat. It is so frustrating."

As we walked, she shared more of her experience with me. "I've always been fat. I was bigger than all of my friends from the time I was little. I was taller too. I've been on more diets and programs than I can count, went to Weight Watchers with my mother from the time I was eleven—all of that. I'm sick of it and don't want to deal with it anymore. This kind of workshop speaks to me because I want to be able to eat mindfully. But I just don't get a sense that the presenter and most of the people in that room get what it is really like for me to live in a body that no one wants to have and that most have spent their lives trying *not* to have."

Even though Nia got some relief by connecting with like-minded others in workshops similar to the one we were attending, she knew that as soon as she left the room to cross the crowded lobby, she'd be subjected to disdainful glances. She'd be judged for how slowly she climbed the stairs leading to the plaza.

"I'm used to it, but it's exhausting," she said to me as we figured out what we wanted for lunch. "I keep making myself go out, but there are times when I can't deal with it and I stay inside. Everyone's got ideas about what I should be doing and assumptions about what I'm not doing. And they feel free to tell me about it."

Worst, she said, is when "I get sucked back into this mindset that there's something wrong with me for not trying to lose weight. There are times when everything I know and trust just flies out the window."

She looked at me tentatively, as I had told her that I was writing a book about Self-led eating. "I don't want to presume, but I'd bet you haven't ever been fat. It is a very different reality."

I confirmed Nia's assumption. I've never been fat, though earlier in my life, parts of me would have said otherwise. While I was occasionally called fat as a kid and was briefly harassed by a group of boys for being "too fat" to date while I was in college, I haven't actually ever been fat. And, in my current life, I don't know what it's like to face scorn and knee-jerk reactions based on my body size. I expect to be able to go out to eat, shop, travel, and meet people without being judged or discriminated against. I can go to the doctor without having to brace myself for the inevitable discussion about needing to lose weight when I go in for my annual physical or need help for a sore throat. I've never had to worry about whether my body size will factor into whether or not I'll get a job or whether I'll be able to find clothes to wear. While I've felt pain related to burdens that parts of me have held about my body, I haven't been subject to emotional and physical harm due to my size, shape, or skin color.

Many of us have exiles who long to be witnessed for how awful it was to be teased or bullied in school for how we looked. The shame and anxiety of these early experiences attach to exiles and shape the way we see ourselves. Energy that we might otherwise invest in joyful and creative exploration of the world gets diverted by our protectors to the grind of trying to change our bodies or to disconnect from them. As painful as this may be, it doesn't compare with the suffering that people experience when their bodies are routinely subject to mistreatment because of their race, sexuality, gender expression, size, shape, or ability.

As I've learned more about the many ways in which I've been privileged, I've realized how it has allowed me to remain unaware of or minimize the extent of the hardship others face for what they weigh, how they appear, and how they function. Until relatively recently, I didn't question some of the messages I learned from my family and the dominant culture: that being fat meant being unhappy and unhealthy, for example, and that if I worked hard enough, I could have the type of body I wanted—fit, healthy, and attractive—and that would make me happier.

When we consider the concept of privilege as "a set of unearned benefits given to people who fit into a specific social group" (Ferguson, 2014), we tend to focus on the advantages one gets from belonging to a dominant group: access to wealth, education, health care, employment, and safety. IFS offers a different way to understand social power. From an IFS perspective, privilege means *not* having exiles who carry wounds due to being a member of a marginalized group. It means not having protectors who constantly have to look out for harm from the dominant culture. It is the ability to remain unaware of the vast ocean of bias because you live in calmer waters. As Sonya Renee Taylor (2021) states, "People who have been slapped by some waves can tell you how hard the waves are on top, right? They can tell you how rough the sea is."

Nia understood this too well. She was exhausted by years of negotiating her own and others' judgments. While she felt good about the work she'd done to heal internally, she could sometimes feel despairing and pessimistic about much change happening in the outside world.

Recently, after a particularly challenging moment with a colleague at work, she emailed me, speaking on behalf of a hopeless part. This hopelessness had been activated by a colleague's casual comment about what Nia was eating for lunch. "She noticed my sandwich and launched into a whole 'Oh, it's so great that you can eat a sandwich like that for lunch. I could never do that!'"

While this kind of intrusion wasn't new to Nia—she was accustomed to others' judgmental comments or glances—she hadn't expected it to come from this colleague.

As Nia gave voice to her hopelessness, I noticed I had parts who felt sad and angry about how often Nia was subjected to this kind of behavior. I also noticed parts who could feel despair about how challenging it is to shift people's perspectives when it comes to fat and health. While most people I know have parts who conceptually agree that anti-fat bias is unjust, they also have parts who are preoccupied to some degree with disliking their bodies and wanting to lose weight. This often unsolicited yet pervasive opposition in our felt beliefs about our bodies is an important polarization to explore.

My own long and challenging exploration has led me to unburden many of the parts of myself who took on negative beliefs about my body or used my dissatisfaction with my body to distract me from other pain.

A major catalyst in this healing process has been what I've learned from my clients and from the people around me who are dedicated to making the world safer for bodies of all kinds (see appendix B for a list of some of the resources I've found helpful). They helped me see how the critical part of myself, who whispered to me from the sidelines and occasionally sucker punched me, wasn't just a nuisance but a symptom of a much larger problem. While the work I did personally wouldn't do much to make the world safer for those who are harmed the most by cultural or legacy burdens, it helped me get clear that I needed to take action. It is my hope that this book will alert others, especially people like me who have not had to live with the same kind of threats to our well-being, of the need to do this kind of work on themselves.

The inclination to bring Self-leadership to external systems is a natural outcome of becoming more Self-led internally. When you become more Self-led, you come to realize that you're a member of a larger system of parts, and when one member of the system is burdened, it reverberates throughout the entire system (Schwartz, 2021). In this Self-led state, you can no longer look past or minimize the real harm that the dominant culture's burdens cause for so many people. You will seek to contribute to others' healing as you heal yourself. As Richard Schwartz (2021) describes it, you "become increasingly prompted to take action on behalf of healing humanity and healing our planet" (p. 134).

Identifying Opportunities to Address or Disrupt Harm in External Systems

Get Curious About and Acknowledge Your Privilege and Bias

While we're all impacted by anti-fat attitudes, we are not all affected in the same way or to the same degree. The extent to which you are affected depends on a number of factors, including your body size and shape, race, gender, age, sexual orientation, ability, and socioeconomic status. There are three levels of anti-fat bias that derive from cultural legacy burdens around fatness that may help you understand how you've been affected: intrapersonal, interpersonal, and institutional (Tovar, 2017).

Intrapersonal or internalized anti-fat bias involves having parts who feel ashamed or inadequate for not being thin enough or looking the way you "should." This affects most of us, since no one can avoid absorbing toxic beliefs about their body in the dominant culture. While intrapersonal anti-fat bias leaves parts of you feeling like you don't measure up, it may or may not align with how others regard and treat your body.

In contrast, *interpersonal* anti-fat bias involves being subjected to comments or negative reactions (e.g., rejection or discrimination) due to your body's shape or size. Nia's experience of receiving judgmental looks at the conference, as well as her colleague's comments about her eating, are good examples of this kind of anti-fat bias.

Institutional anti-fat bias relates to how valued you feel by the larger culture and the degree to which you feel like your participation and existence are welcome. This sense of belonging gets communicated in many different ways: through access to quality medical care, educational and job opportunities, legal protection from discrimination, and respectful, positive representation in movies and literature.

In a 2022 article, Danish comedian, author, and fat activist Sofie Hagen described the relief she experienced during the coronavirus pandemic. Her writing provides a vivid example of the impact of institutional anti-fat bias: "Quarantine was the only time in my adult life where I hadn't felt the stress of 'can I fit into this seat?' or the painful, pinching feelings of the armrests digging into my hips, cutting off blood supply to my legs. Suddenly, there were no plane seats, tube seats, café seats, waiting room seats, or—yes—toilet seats. Or toilet stalls. [...] Many of us fat people experienced what it was like to not be abused in the street or feel unwelcome in public spaces."

Your reactions to Hagen's personal account of what it's like to navigate the world as a fat person can tell you a lot about your privilege and your biases. You're privileged if you've never had to think about the seating in a restaurant, theater, plane, bus, or waiting room and whether it will support you, if you don't anticipate being turned down for a job because of your size, or if you expect to find what you need when you shop for clothes or go to the doctor (e.g., appropriately sized blood pressure cuffs or MRI tables). While you may know what it's like to be harassed in the street, especially if you're a woman, you don't know what it's like to be publicly abused or excluded in these ways because of your size.

If you can relate to Hagen's description, you may notice some relief at having someone articulate what you've experienced yourself. But if her account offers a new perspective, you may notice parts who have a variety of responses. Parts of you may feel judgmental (e.g., "If she just lost some weight . . ."), uneasy or fearful (e.g., "I would hate to get like that"), or even contemptuous (e.g., "Why should we have to accommodate people who refuse to take care of themselves?"). Each of these reactions reflects anti-fat bias. If you found yourself reacting in any of these ways, here are a couple of questions to ask:

- Can you get curious about the parts of yourself who hold these beliefs?

- If you can, see if it's possible for them to let you know what's behind their hatred of or fear of fatness.

    ○ Where did they get these beliefs?

    ○ Which parts of you do they protect?

    ○ What would they need from you to hold these beliefs less tightly so you, from Self, could unburden them?

- If you're having trouble getting curious, you're blended with parts who hold anti-fat bias or who are ashamed of the ones who hold the bias. Each of these are important trailheads for you to explore. Aubrey Gordon (2023), in her book *"You Just Need to Lose Weight": And 19 Other Myths About Fat People*, offers reflections and recommendations for disrupting bias that can help you further identify the anti-fat beliefs that parts of you hold.

Detecting Parts Who Engage in Social Comparison

Noticing the parts of yourself who feel superior or inferior is a good way to identify parts who still need healing in your system. If you feel virtuous or more "together" when you eat (or don't eat) certain foods or engage in certain kinds of exercise, or if you feel better than others because you work as many hours as you do, you have parts who need your help. The same holds for parts who feel inferior or less worthy because of the way they eat, move, rest, and function. Not only will the burdens each of these parts carry continue to cause you pain, they will also limit or prevent you from being able to see or do anything to mitigate others' pain.

If you notice parts who feel guilty about the biases carried by other parts of you and the harm they've inflicted, internally or externally, let them know you see them. Remind them that these burdens are not *intrinsic* to those other parts. With the cooperation of the parts who feel shame and guilt, you have the ability to do something about them now. Every time you pause parts who are judging or making assumptions about yourself or someone else, and with each unburdening of these parts, you create the potential for a ripple effect that helps others do the same.

Remind these parts that there are many others to whom they can look to for inspiration and guidance, people who are using their lived experiences and knowledge to create a world that is safer for more bodies.

Learning from these people can help your parts become more open as they consider perspectives that challenge what they've been led to believe.

A Few Words About "All Parts Are Welcome"

This basic principle of the IFS model is that all parts are inherently valuable in spite of the burdens they carry or the roles they've been forced to take on. That said, burdened parts can cause harm because of the bias they hold *when you blend with and speak from their perspective*. For example, when a part of you laments "I'm so fat!" in a group of friends or an online post, you are perpetuating the toxic belief that fat is bad.

Each of us can take responsibility for becoming aware of our parts, do the work that is required to unburden them, and in so doing, perpetuate less harm. "All parts are welcome" is thus an invitation to heal, rather than to exile, the parts of yourself who carry bias by reducing the shame and blame (internal and external) that arise when you confuse parts with their burdens.

"All parts are welcome" doesn't mean you have to like or welcome someone else's parts. If you have been hurt by the unconscious or conscious bias of others' parts, it can be quite challenging to remember or care about the other person's internal system and whatever their parts are negotiating. That makes sense. From Self, you can extend compassion to your parts for their pain and hopelessness about things ever changing. Depending on the source of the insult, you may choose to speak on behalf of the parts who got hurt or find a way to set a boundary with the other person to limit further harm. It may also help to speak with someone who can understand the harm that you experienced or to join communities that view anti-fatness through a social justice lens and that offer inclusive and safe spaces in which to do your healing (e.g., the Center for Body Trust and others listed in appendix B).

In essence, "All parts are welcome as long as you're with them" (T. Herbine-Blank, personal communication, May 24, 2021). When you unblend from and take care of your own parts, you increase the likelihood of right action, taking the steps to disrupt bias or make a repair when you've been hurtful.

Get Informed and Stay Curious

Over twenty-five years ago, Becky W. Thompson (1994) wrote the following in *A Hunger So Wide and So Deep*: "In a country brimming with glorified images of youth, whiteness, thinness, and wealth, it makes painful sense that dissatisfaction with appearance often serves as a stand-in for topics that are still invisible" (p. 11). This statement is equally relevant today.

Over the last few years, as we've navigated the pandemic, experienced the Black Lives Matter and #MeToo movements, and witnessed the overturning of *Roe v. Wade*, we've watched vulnerable parts of ourselves activate protectors who remain highly polarized: us/them, right/wrong, compassion/hate. Each of these critical junctures has given us opportunities to reflect on how differently groups of people are treated in the dominant culture.

The pandemic in particular laid bare how cultural and legacy burdens dictate narratives about bodies and health. The majority of reports proclaiming that BIPOC and fat people are more susceptible to dying of COVID, for example, failed to mention or consider the social determinants of health that might explain the observed disparities, chief among them stress and lack of access to adequate health care.

The systemic bias that drives this misrepresentation is long-standing. As Sabrina Strings (2019) explains when she describes the racist roots of diet culture in *Fearing the Black Body*, anti-fat attitudes emerged as a strategy to bolster White privilege and justify enslavement during the slave trade. Race "scientists" deemed fatness as a key indicator of the inferiority of Black people, whom they judged as less rational and in control of their appetites. Similarly, Da'Shaun L. Harrison's work (2021) has explored how the "War on Obesity" was based on scientific studies that were deeply flawed by implicitly continuing to utilize ideas about fat inferiority as a stand-in for racial difference.

More recently, Katherine Flegal (2021) published an account of how the results of her research exploring the relationship between weight and mortality were questioned and distorted for over fifteen years. By loosening the association between fat and poor health outcomes, she touched a cultural nerve. Personally and professionally attacked when her results failed to support biased narratives about health and fat, her disturbing experience again reflects how intrapersonal and interpersonal anti-fatness perpetuate institutional anti-fatness. Once more, the question is: What makes large bodies dangerous to the degree that a war is declared on them? Are any of us truly safe if our bodies could lead us to be exiled and reviled?

The casualties of the War on Obesity are impossible to estimate, as this battle rages on. However, one indication of the harm done may be the increased incidence of eating disorders, which has been documented since the turn of the century (Galmiche et al., 2019). Evelyn Tribole (2019), the cofounder of Intuitive Eating, attributes this increase to dieting and body dissatisfaction, as she states that "the normalization of diet culture, masquerading as wellness, health, or lifestyle is creating the conditions for eating disorders to manifest and thrive." While true, this observation captures the tip of the iceberg. As Jessica Wilson (2023) notes, the recently popular notion of "diet culture" fails to acknowledge the deeper impact of racism and social inequity on the relationships we have with our bodies.

From an IFS perspective, the conditions Tribole and Wilson refer to fuel the fear and shame that drive managers to critique or control your eating and get you to change your body. These strategies activate firefighters to ease the deprivation or distract from the painful feelings that come from being made to go hungry or believing something is terribly wrong with you. Problems arise when you make the firefighters the problem rather than addressing the underlying pain that motivates the behavior. As Schwartz and Sweezy (2020) note, "Wars against firefighters at any human system level are consistently disastrous. Either the firefighters escalate and symptoms worsen, or managers succeed in repressing the firefighter behavior (temporarily) by imposing a rigid police state" (p. 248).

A considerable amount of research attests to the impact of police states on bodies, whether they result from other people who believe your body is a problem or from the parts of yourself who have absorbed these beliefs. Interpersonal discrimination of all kinds is associated with psychological and physiological disturbances (e.g., elevations in blood pressure, cholesterol, C-reactive protein, blood glucose, and cortisol levels) that contribute to a variety of health issues, including hypertension, cardiovascular disease, diabetes, respiratory problems, and low birth weight (Richman et al., 2017). For example, a recent study asked Black adults to document incidents of overt racial discrimination and microaggressions as they occurred in real time and also to provide saliva samples four times a day over the study period (Nam et al., 2022). Results showed that participants' cortisol levels nearly doubled the morning after they experienced racial discrimination and increased on the same day when they experienced microaggressions. Since elevated cortisol has been implicated in a number of serious illnesses, these results support the idea that overt racism and more subtle experiences of discrimination have a detrimental impact on health.

This appears to be the case for stigma related to weight. While the dominant culture and medical science have taken the correlation between fatness and medical symptoms and made it causal, a growing body of research has pointed to the unique role that weight stigma may play in the development of these problems.

It wouldn't be surprising if you notice skeptical parts piping up as you consider the possibility that negative health outcomes for higher-weight people might be attributable to factors other than fatness. You're so accustomed to hearing things like "You can't be fat and fit," and how fatness leads to higher rates of illness and death. However, as reviews of existing research document, there's ample evidence to suggest that while higher weight can contribute to health issues, the relationship is much more complex than is typically portrayed, and weight stigma appears to figure prominently in that relationship (Manne, 2024; Sole-Smith, 2023; Tomiyama, 2018). Witnessing weight stigma has been shown to result in elevated cortisol levels for lean and higher-weight participants alike (Schvey et al., 2014). A study by Sutin and colleagues (2017) suggests that judgments related to weight need not be overt to have a negative impact on the body. Their study showed that children whose parents perceived them to be "overweight" (i.e., had parts who judged their children for weighing more than they "should") had higher levels of C-reactive protein—an inflammation marker—in their blood. This was true regardless of a child's actual BMI, indicating that parental perception of weight, as opposed to weight itself, was responsible for these physiological changes. While these findings are correlational, it isn't hard to imagine that having a parent who harbors negative beliefs about your body would feel bad or threatening and have a visceral impact.

Equally unsurprising are studies that indicate that having a part inside your own system who holds judgments about your body negatively impacts your emotional and physical well-being. Robinson and Sutin (2017) found that children perceived as "overweight" by their parents in early childhood gain more weight by early adolescence than children whose parents perceive then as "normal" weight—because the children take on the belief that they are "overweight" and engage in more dieting. Himmelstein and colleagues (2015) found that, independent of women's actual BMI, those who believed they were "heavy" displayed sustained elevations in cortisol after being exposed to weight-stigmatizing messages relative to women who believed they were of "average" weight. Pearl and colleagues (2017) also demonstrated that individuals with internalized anti-fatness (i.e., believing they were lazy or unattractive because of their weight) were three times more likely to have metabolic syndrome and six times more likely to have high triglycerides than their "low internalized weight bias counterparts" (p. 58).

As Virginia Sole-Smith (2023) notes, some obesity researchers have recently been more open to acknowledging the role that weight stigma plays in the health issues that have commonly been blamed on weight. She relates weight stigma researcher Rebecca Puhl's framing of weight stigma as a form of chronic stress that affects us physiologically as well as psychologically.

In Kate Manne's (2024) delineation of the various ways weight stigma may mediate the relationship between weight and health, she highlights how internalized weight bias can lead to behaviors that can contribute to adverse health outcomes, among them weight cycling and avoiding situations that might result in more harm (e.g., exercising in public, medical care). I've certainly witnessed this in my own practice. In addition to engaging in chronic dieting, many of my clients avoid exercise, annual physicals, and other medical exams due to their fear of being told to lose weight or being humiliated. From an IFS perspective, it makes sense that protectors would mobilize to do whatever they can to minimize the likelihood of being hurt.

Taking a cue from Marquisele Mercedes and Monica Kriete (2023) and Ragen Chastain (2023), I want to point out that the aforementioned studies on weight stigma focused on understanding stigma as it contributes to the undesirable outcome of fatness. My intention is not to perpetuate that idea but to underscore how cultural legacy burdens cause significant physical and emotional distress that is passed along to others—as Gordon (and Schwartz) point out—like a virus.

Whether stigma impacts health via prolonged nervous system activation, restricted access to or avoidance of supportive resources (e.g., health insurance, attuned medical care, housing, psychotherapy, legal services), or the tendency to cope with stigma by engaging in coping behaviors that can have harmful downsides, it is clear that biased beliefs wreak havoc on our bodies. To learn more about how burdened parts impact physical and psychological well-being, see *Internal Family Systems Therapy for Physical Health and Illness* (Sowell et al., in press).

Engage in Self-Led Action to Prevent or Offset Harm

As you've seen in the case vignettes throughout this book, cultural and legacy burdens are personally experienced and intimately felt. They touch your deepest experience of being in a body. They affect how you regard and treat yourself and the people around you. As you become more aware of the biases in your system, as well as the work you can do to heal them, you'll become more interested in doing what you can to disrupt bias when you witness it occurring around you.

For example, friends and clients often tell me about their latest diet. Since they know my stance regarding intentional weight loss, they'll often lead with something like "I know you probably think this isn't good, but I just need to get off sugar" and proceed to tell me the tedious details of the latest plan. They'll usually follow this with some kind of justification, such as "I think it's reasonable to want to be healthy" or "I can't just eat what I want if I want to look the way I want to look."

I work to get curious as they describe their intentions, especially if this is a monthly or seasonal conversation. I stay clear about what I believe—that Self-led relationships with food and the body are more likely to enhance emotional and physical well-being because they are compassionate and attuned, and thus more sustainable—and speak to it if I'm asked. What I don't want is to create an alternative police state in which parts who dwell on weight loss or changing the body are viewed as bad. There are so many reasons why people get pulled into dieting, changing, or hiding their bodies: traumas of various kinds, physical changes due to injury or aging, discrimination regarding sexuality and gender, financial stress, or political unrest. Therefore, I try to engage people's curiosity about their decisions. What are they hoping for and what's driving them? Which parts believe losing weight would help and why? How has this worked (and not worked) for them in the past?

Of course, it can be more challenging for me to remain Self-led when conversations shift from dieting to interventions that have long-ranging—sometimes irreversible or unknown—physical and emotional consequences (e.g., bariatric surgery, weight-loss drugs). Aside from the use of these interventions with children—which, in my view, clearly violates principles of body autonomy and informed consent—I work to get curious with the individual struggling with these decisions and their particular context. While I may have strong beliefs about what is best for them as well as fears about how they will be impacted by these procedures and drugs, *I do not live in their body*. I do not know the complex matrix of historical burdens and current physical and emotional realities that are coming to bear on their decision. Rather than cling tightly to one (apprehensive, righteous, or judgmental) pole of the debate, I work to get my parts to give me some room so I can be curious about and *engage the other person's curiosity* about the proposed intervention. I keep in mind the importance of doing what I can to reduce the shame and blame associated with these conversations so that the other person will be more likely to consider the various risks and benefits involved instead of being prematurely shut down by parts who fear my parts' judgment or concern.

When I'm with a group of friends and the conversation turns to diets or, more recently in my cohort, anti-aging treatments, I will often change the subject, sometimes with an explicit acknowledgment of what I'm doing. However, there are times when I'm tired or when there's a group vibe that feels difficult to interrupt and I end up engaging for a few minutes. After a long week of Zoom meetings, for example, I may notice a part who will make a comment or two about my neck or crow's feet. When this happens, I pause the part who can get critical of myself for going there and remind it that my appearance-focused parts just need a little more support from me.

Changing your behavior in social situations can be challenging, even more so when it involves shifting deeply ingrained beliefs about health and wellness.

A colleague recently related her confusion about not giving weight-loss or fitness-focused compliments. "It feels bad to me to not say anything when I know someone's been trying to get in shape or lose weight."

A thoughtful woman who is known for being highly sensitive, she has found it hard to absorb that these comments perpetuate anti-fat bias. This example illustrates an important challenge—how to be sensitive to individual pain and needs while remaining aware of and working to disrupt the cultural biases that continue to perpetuate harm. Nowhere is this more relevant than in recent discourses regarding the use of glucagon-like peptide (GLP-1) receptor agonists (e.g., Ozempic), medications that were initially developed to treat diabetes and were subsequently found to produce significant weight loss. These drugs can be helpful and even lifesaving for some people, but they can also exacerbate biases about weight and health.

To put it simply, positioning fatness as an inherently unhealthy and undesirable condition that can and should be eradicated by a pill or injection will keep people subject to discrimination and at war with their own parts. If a "solution" to fatness exists, shouldn't all large-bodied people take advantage of it? What, then, about those who remain fat—are they "not taking care of themselves"? Will they be judged as "lazy" or "unwilling" to give up their "addictions" to "bad" food?

What if we, instead, pause and get curious about our reactivity? There's a lot we don't yet know about these treatments. We don't know if they have serious long-term side effects. As some speculate, data from existing clinical trials involving thousands of subjects over a period of months may not adequately capture the kinds of adverse effects associated with these drugs as the scale and duration of use rise—in other words, after millions of people have used the drugs for years (Gou & Schwartz, 2023).

What we do know is that these drugs don't work for everyone, and they can have serious and intolerable side effects in the short term. We know that they don't result in permanent weight loss. Once the user discontinues them, they can expect swift weight regain, thus contributing to the adverse impacts of weight cycling. In addition to feeling out of control due to the rapid weight regain, people can feel overwhelmed by the resurgence of intense hunger that drives parts to binge as their body fights to regain the lost weight. The despair and self-recrimination that follow are all too familiar for the folks who take these medications.

Weight stigma is so pernicious that it's easy to understand why people would be willing to tolerate the considerable costs associated with weight loss medications (e.g., loss of enjoyment in food, nausea and other unpleasant side effects, potential long-term risks) in order to escape the shame and abuse they get from others and from parts of themselves.

While weight loss may alleviate shame for some parts, other parts who carry burdens related to fatness will continue to suffer. They will worry about being judged for taking the medications or fear what may happen if they aren't able to access them in the future or if they stop working.

It's also easy to see how the proliferation of weight loss drugs will amplify the cultural legacy burdens related to fatness, health, race, and class. Weight loss drugs are not accessible for many people. Issues of accessibility and affordability hit members of marginalized groups hardest—those who already shoulder systemic bias and social inequities that cause so much physical and emotional harm in the first place.

From the perspective of Unburdened Eating, the challenge is to do our own work so we don't get stuck in good-or-bad binaries and instead address the root of the problem, the parts of ourselves who judge our own and others' bodies for *whatever* reason so we can remain clear about what needs to be done to effect change for all of us. Otherwise, as McMillan Cottom (2023) writes, "We can create drugs that help people lose weight, but the conditions for making some people undesirable—at a cost—will still be lurking in the shadows."

Although it may feel overwhelming to consider all the work that needs to be done to address the toxic beliefs and practices that keep us hyper-focused on or disconnected from our bodies, I offer this simple reminder: You play an important role in disrupting bias instead of perpetuating it or making it worse. Every time you choose to get curious about your beliefs and reactions to what's being said or written about food, health, and bodies—every time you speak from Self instead of criticizing or shaming yourself or others for how they look, behave, and function—you contribute to the healing of the larger system. To the degree that you get to know and heal your own parts, you add to the Self-energy that will make a difference on the collective level.

If you're a doctor, dietitian, or mental health professional, recognize that what you do and say (or don't) has a significant impact on your clients. Many people avoid getting medical care because of the painful assumptions, misdiagnoses, and lack of care they have received earlier in their lives. Several of my clients have had their restriction overlooked or minimized due to their body size. They've met with clinicians who have either promoted weight loss or viewed it as a goal of successful treatment. Other clients have seen their preoccupation with weight and exercise become the focus of treatment while their primary issue was overlooked (e.g., struggles with sexual or gender identity). In an article in *Essence* magazine, Dr. Whitney Trotter, a psychiatric nurse practitioner, registered dietitian, and co-founder of the BIPoC Eating Disorders Conference, discusses how biases related to race and weight skew clinicians' assessments of BIPOC individuals, adding to long-standing mistrust of and frustration with the medical system and the field of eating disorders (Ayoola, 2023).

It's important to stay curious about your assumptions. Sand Chang (2022, as cited in Kinavey & Sturtevant, 2022), an IFS trainer and Body Trust® provider, notes that the behaviors we associate with disordered eating among cisgender people can mean something quite different for transgender individuals: "It may look similar on the outside in terms of *behaviors* such as food restriction, binge eating, compulsive exercise, or purging. But what's on the *inside* is different. It's rarely about wanting our bodies to look a certain way just for aesthetics or desirability. It's about safety" (p. 64). The eating disorder behaviors that can seem extreme or out of control might actually be attempts to get agency over how one is perceived in order to avoid being harmed.

The focus on appearance and observable behavior versus internal distress leaves many people in chronic, unacknowledged, and untreated (either not diagnosed or not covered by insurance) pain. This includes men whose bingeing behavior is often overlooked or normalized. This is why I don't use DSM criteria to identify eating disorders or disordered eating. Too often, such criteria reflect cultural biases regarding eating and bodies instead of the actual experience of my clients, as when restriction is minimized or as when restriction is disbelieved in my larger clients.

Educating yourself and getting consultation so you don't per-petuate cultural stereotypes is vital to providing ethical, attuned care. Normalizing the physical changes associated with developmental stages (e.g., puberty, pregnancy, menopause, aging), foregoing the use of BMI as an indicator of health, and not relying on weight to diagnose eating disorders would be a few ways to mitigate harm. Not automatically associating fatness with depression or a trauma history is another. (See Matz, 2022, for her important discussion of the latter assumption.)

If you're a therapist, keep in mind that many people avoid getting help for their eating issues, not only because of their own shame and fear of judgment but also because their previous therapists haven't engaged them in explorations about their relationships with food and their bodies. Amazingly, most of my clients report that they've spent years in treatment without ever speaking about their bodies. It's important to get to know the parts of yourself who refrain from having these discussions with clients and learn why they do this. Do your own burdens related to food and the body prevent you from recognizing them in others? Do parts of you worry about being seen as ignorant or racist as you make space for these explorations with your clients, especially those with intersecting, marginalized identities? Even when you have some ideas of the kinds of questions that would help you be more culturally sensitive (see Small, 2021), parts of you may need reassurance from your Self or help to unburden before they will let you take the risk to engage in these conversations. Appendix B includes some resources for health professionals who are interested in becoming more aware of the impact of their biases on their clients.

Similarly, if you're a parent, aunt, uncle, grandparent, coach, teacher, youth group leader, or mentor, you have a prime opportunity to prevent or alleviate the shame that takes hold early and requires so much work to heal down the road. Many of my clients remember a single negative comment that someone in authority made about their body, which set them up for years of disordered eating. Their exiles tell stories about being teased, judged, abused, or ogled by trusted adults, admonished by doctors and teachers, and excluded from teams, clubs, and theater productions because of how their bodies looked or how they functioned. They remember being judged or stereotyped because of their race, sexuality, gender identity, and socioeconomic status.

If being judged for being fat lasts a lifetime, so does its opposite. My clients remember the teacher who noticed them when others did not, the coach who praised their effort instead of their appearance or performance, and the nurse or doctor who reassured them that their stretch marks were not their fault. They remember the loved ones who took them out for ice cream or shared the joy of making meals together. Positive input from someone who holds a meaningful position in a young person's life is often a powerful inoculation against future shame.

This awareness led Christina to recognize that her relationship with her nephew could provide an important counterpoint to her brother and sister-in-law's preoccupation with dieting and exercise. When her nephew announced that he intended to cut out "white foods," for example, she got curious and asked him about his decision rather than arguing with him. She asked him what made him believe white foods weren't good for him and if he noticed how he felt when he did eat these foods. Because she'd grown up with this type of thinking, Christina noticed parts who reacted with alarm and some irritation at her nephew's proposal. But she got them to ease up so she could listen to him without judgment, which engaged his curiosity. She also modeled balance in her choices regarding exercise and food. If you are looking for resources to help you prevent or disrupt anti-fat bias, Virginia Sole-Smith's (2023) compelling book *Fat Talk: Parenting in the Age of Diet Culture* offers many helpful suggestions.

Changing the systemic biases that keep so many people in pain will take a good deal of hard work and Self-energy for generations to come. When it feels daunting, I take heart in the fact that the work we do internally impacts the external world in countless small and sometimes large ways. It allows us to liberate our parts to be who they were designed to be so that they can take on new, more expansive, and joyful roles that fit their talents. (See the following mandala, which depicts the potential unburdened system; Pastor, 2013). Self-energy calls forth Self-energy in others. This is one way change happens, ending micro- and macroaggressions against our bodies and those of others. Like many IFS therapists and coaches, I anchor myself in the 8 Cs, particularly curiosity, compassion, and clarity, to cultivate the courage to live what Valarie Kaur (2017) calls "revolutionary love, the choice to enter into labor for others who do not look like us, for our opponents who hurt us, and for ourselves."

The Unburdened Internal System

Unburdened Managers

Take on a balanced approach to daily responsibilities. Are effective & collaborative, encouraging other parts and people. Advocate for growth & contributing talents. Can be lovingly parental and nurturing.

Confident Cooperative Clear Discerning Helpful Creative in Problem Solving Competent Calm

Self Energy

Easily flows between & through parts, is more readily in the lead & assisted by parts. Embodies mindfulness. Is grounded in the present moment, holding a perspective broader than the parts'. Is able to heal/comfort parts & speak for them. Is inherently curious & compassionate about people & parts. Is able to act courageously & with an open heart.

Connected Calm Intuitive Creative Accepting Compassionate Curious Clear Confident

Unburdened Firefighters

Signal Self directly when stress levels are high. Use effective self-soothing activities & diversions. Add spice to life with passion & adventure, healthy risk-taking & humor. Advocate for fairness & stand up to injustices. Lend courage & confidence to act bravely in challenging situations.

Courageous Adventurous Confident Passionate Creative Sensual Fun

Unburdened Exiles

Are tender and sensitive parts with childlike curiosity and delight, advocating for connection & care. Feel secure with Self as primary caretaker, feeling freer to reach out to others. Offer intuitions about others' feelings. Enjoy being open & trusting.

Tender Playful Spontaneous Open Curious Trusting Sensitive Warm Innocent

The Self-led person looks and acts comfortable in her own being, interacting with others from integrated parts and awareness. Parts work more harmoniously together with fewer burdens causing them to overreact. Many parts may be released from protective roles, while others will effectively protect only when needed. Over time, the person is less easily destabilized and better able to recover from challenges in general. The inherent gifts of each part are more available, weaving in and out consciously. A Self-led person brings an abiding sense of curiosity, acceptance, and openheartedness to their relationships, naturally inviting others' Self energy to increase. Self energy flows seamlessly within a person, with a sense of connectedness to the Self energy that surrounds him.

Text by Mariel Pastor, LMFT with Richard Schwartz, PhD
Original graphic by Jan Mullen LCSW
©2013 All rights reserved. Unauthorized duplication prohibited. www.MarielPastor.com

Appendix A

IFS Resources

Books

- Anderson, F. (2021). *Transcending trauma: Healing complex PTSD with Internal Family Systems therapy*. PESI Publishing.

- Anderson, F., Sweezy, M., & Schwartz, R. C. (2017). *Internal Family Systems skills training manual: Trauma-informed treatment for anxiety, depression, PTSD & substance abuse*. PESI Publishing.

- Floyd, T. (2024). *Listening when parts speak: A practical guide to healing with Internal Family Systems therapy and ancestor wisdom*. Hay House, Inc.

- Gutiérrez, N. Y. (2022). *The pain we carry: Healing from complex PTSD for people of color*. New Harbinger Publications.

- McConnell, S. (2020). *Somatic Internal Family Systems therapy: Awareness, breath, resonance, movement, and touch in practice*. North Atlantic Books.

- Riemersma, J., & Schwartz, R. C. (Eds.). (2023). *Altogether us: Integrating the IFS model with key modalities, communities, and trends*. Pivotal Press.

- Schwartz, R. C. (2008). *You're the one you've been waiting for: Bringing courageous love to intimate relationships*. Center for Self Leadership.

- Schwartz, R. C. (2021). *No bad parts: Healing trauma and restoring wholeness with the Internal Family Systems model*. Sounds True Publications.

- Schwartz, R. S. (2023). *Introduction to Internal Family Systems*. Sounds True Publications.

- Schwartz, R. C., & Sweezy, M. (2020). *Internal Family Systems therapy* (2nd ed.). Guilford Press.

- Sowell, N., Sweezy, M., & Schwartz, R. C. (in press). *Internal Family Systems therapy for physical health and illness: Healing the underlying stress, shame, and trauma*. PESI Publishing.

- Sweezy, M. (2023). *Internal Family Systems therapy for shame and guilt*. Guilford Press.

- Sweezy, M., & Ziskind, E. L. (Eds.). (2016). *Innovations and elaborations in Internal Family Systems therapy*. Routledge.

- Sykes, C., Sweezy, M., & Schwartz, R. C. (2023). *Internal Family Systems therapy for addiction: Trauma-informed, compassion-based interventions for substance use, eating, gambling and more*. PESI Publishing.

Audiovisual Resources

Available online free of charge:

- *All Parts Welcome*: A conversation with Richard Schwartz and Elizabeth Gilbert on how IFS can support creativity, spirituality, and prayer (https://www.youtube.com/watch?v=VBYrJOK4Dtk)

- *Fire Drill Meditation*: A guided meditation from Richard Schwartz to help you unblend when you get activated by someone (https://www.youtube.com/watch?v=JQ91WpwODWo)

- *IFS by Dr. Richard Schwartz*: A series of meditations on InsightTimer with Richard Schwartz (https://insighttimer.com/meditation-playlists/PzDHxxWwi1L9dVJVvGaV)

- *IFS Polarization Demo*: A discussion with Richard Schwartz on how to work with a polarization (https://youtu.be/Al7jnW-Z08w)

- *Intro to Internal Family Systems (IFS)*: A detailed introduction to IFS with Richard Schwartz (https://youtu.be/6X45Y74blSg)

- *The Path Meditation*: A guided meditation with Richard Schwartz to give you a sense of unblending and the experience of Self/Self-energy (https://www.youtube.com/watch?v=kWEoHSe1zGw)

- *No Bad Parts:* A detailed introduction to IFS with Richard Schwartz and Tami Simon (https://youtu.be/zb6RMXknil8)

- *Unblend and ANS Review*: An illustration of the process of unblending with Toni Herbine-Blank (https://youtu.be/WKyHC6wVgAA)
- *Understanding Our Inner Critic*: A demonstration of getting to know a critical part with Richard Schwartz (https://youtu.be/Ar8PbATergE)

Available for purchase:

- *Greater Than the Sum of Our Parts*: A six-session audio course with Richard Schwartz that includes many meditations and experiential exercises designed to help you get to know your internal system (https://www.soundstrue.com/products/greater-than-the-sum-of-our-parts)
- *Meditations for Self*: An audio download including eight guided meditations by Richard Schwartz (https://ifs-institute.com/store/245)

Podcasts

- *Conversations with Alanis Morissette* (Alanis Morissette, episode #9 with Richard Schwartz)
- *The Emotional Eating (and Everything Else) Podcast* (Kim Daniels, PhD)
- *Getting Curious* (Jonathan Van Ness, episode #91 with Richard Schwartz)
- *IFS Talks* (Aníbal Henriques and Tisha Shull)
- *Purely IFS with Emma and Gayle* (Gayle Williamson and Emma Redfern)
- *Ten Percent Happier* (Dan Harris, episode #323 with Richard Schwartz)
- *The One Inside* (Tammy Sollenberger)
- *The Tim Ferriss Show* (Tim Ferriss, episode #492 with Richard Schwartz)
- *We Can Do Hard Things* (Glennon Doyle, epidodes #295 and #296 with Richard Schwartz)

See https://ifs-institute.com for additional articles, videos, books, retreats, workshops, and training opportunities.

Appendix B

Anti-Diet and Body Liberation Resources

Books

- Chang, S. C., Singh, A. A., & dickey, l. m. (2018). *A clinician's guide to gender-affirming care: Working with transgender and gender nonconforming clients.* New Harbinger.

- Cox, J. A. (2020). *Fat girls in Black bodies: Creating communities of our own.* North Atlantic Books.

- Gay, R. (2017). *Hunger: A memoir of (my) body.* HarperCollins.

- Gordon, A. (2020). *What we don't talk about when we talk about fat.* Beacon Press.

- Gordon, A. (2023). *"You just need to lose weight": And 19 other myths about fat people.* Beacon Press.

- Guadiani, J. L. (2018). *Sick enough: A guide to the medical complications of eating disorders.* Routledge.

- Harrison, C. (2021). *Anti-diet: Reclaim your time, money, well-being, and happiness through Intuitive Eating.* Little, Brown Spark.

- Harrison, C. (2023). *The wellness trap: Break free from diet culture, disinformation, and dubious diagnoses, and find your true well-being.* Little, Brown Spark.

- Harrison, D. L. (2021). *Belly of the beast: The politics of anti-fatness as anti-Blackness*. North Atlantic Books.

- Kinavey, H., & Sturtevant, D. (2022). *Reclaiming body trust: A path to healing & liberation*. TarcherPerigee.

- King, C. (2023). *The body liberation project: How understanding racism and diet culture helps cultivate joy and build collective freedom*. Tiny Reparations Books.

- Kinsey, D. (2022). *Decolonizing wellness: A QTBIPOC-centered guide to escape the diet trap, heal your self-image, and achieve body liberation*. BenBella Books.

- Laymon, K. (2018). *Heavy: An American memoir*. Scribner.

- Manne, K. (2024). *Unshrinking: How to face fatphobia*. Crown.

- Matz, J., & Frankel, E. (2024). *Beyond a shadow of a diet* (3rd ed.). Routledge.

- Matz, J., Pershing, A., & Harrison C. (2024). *The emotional eating, chronic dieting, binge eating & body image workbook: A trauma-informed weight-inclusive approach to make peace with food & reduce body shame*. PESI Publishing, Inc.

- Nolan, S. (2021). *Don't let it get you down: Essays on race, gender, and the body*. Simon & Schuster.

- Pausé, C., & Taylor, S. R. (Eds.). (2021). *The Routledge international handbook of fat studies*. Routledge.

- Pershing, A., & Turner, C. (2019). *Binge eating disorder: The journey to recovery and beyond*. Routledge.

- Piran, N. (2017). *Journeys of embodiment at the intersection of body and culture: The developmental theory of embodiment*. Academic Press.

- Riemersma, J. (Ed.). (2023). *Altogether us: Integrating the IFS model with key modalities, communities, and trends*. Pivotal Press.

- Sole-Smith, V. (2018). *The eating instinct: Food culture, body image, and guilt in America*. Henry Holt and Company.

- Sole-Smith, V. (2023). *Fat talk: Parenting in the age of diet culture*. Henry Holt and Company.

- Strings, S. (2019). *Fearing the Black body: The racial origins of fat phobia.* New York University Press.

- Taylor, S. R. (2021). *The body is not an apology: The power of radical self-love* (2nd ed.). Berrett-Koehler Publishers.

- Thompson, B. W. (1994). *A hunger so wide and deep: A multiracial view of women's eating problems.* University of Minnesota Press.

- Wilson, J. (2023). *It's always been ours: Rewriting the story of Black women's bodies.* Hachette Go.

- Wong, A. (Ed.). (2020). *Disability visibility: First-person stories from the twenty-first century.* Vintage Books.

Articles and Chapters

- Calogero, R. M., Tylka, T. L., Mensinger, J. L., Meadows, A., & Daníelsdóttir, S. (2019). Recognizing the fundamental right to be fat: A weight-inclusive approach to size acceptance and healing from sizeism. *Women & Therapy, 42*(1–2), 22–44. https://doi.org/10.1080/02703149.2018.1524067

- Catanzaro, J. (2017). IFS and eating disorders: Healing the parts who hide in plain sight. In M. Sweezy & E. L. Ziskind (Eds.), *Innovations and elaborations in Internal Family Systems therapy* (pp. 49–69). Routledge.

- Catanzaro, J. (2022). Trusting Self to heal: Removing constraints to therapists' self- energy transforms their treatment of eating disordered clients. In E. E. Redfern (Ed.), *Internal Family Systems therapy: Supervision and consultation* (pp. 94–108). Routledge.

- Kinavey, H., & Cool, C. (2019). The broken lens: How anti-fat bias in psychotherapy is harming our clients and what to do about it. *Women & Therapy, 42*(1–2), 116–130. https://doi.org/10.1080/02703149.2018.1524070

- Mercedes, M. (2020, September 16). The unbearable whiteness and fatphobia of "anti-diet" dietitians. *Medium.* https://marquisele.medium.com/the-unbearable-whiteness-and-fatphobia-of-anti-diet-dietitians-f3d07fab717d

- McHugh, M. C., & Chrisler, J. C. (2019). Making space for every body: Ending sizeism in psychotherapy and training. *Women & Therapy, 42* (1–2), 7–21. https://doi.org/10.1080/02703149.2018.1524062
- Piran, N. (2016). Embodied paths in aging: Body journeys towards enhanced agency and self-attunement. *Women & Therapy, 39*(1–2), 186–201. https://doi.org/10.1080/02703149.2016.1116853
- Smith, C. A. (2019). Intersectionality and sizeism: Implications for mental health practitioners. *Women & Therapy, 42*(1–2), 59–78. https://doi.org /10.1080/02703149.2018.1524076

Podcasts

- *Burnt Toast* (Virginia Sole-Smith)
- *Dietitians Unplugged* (Aaron Flores and Glenys Oyston)
- *Fierce Fatty* (Vinny Welsby)
- *Food Heaven* (Wendy Lopez and Jessica Jones)
- *Food Psych*® (Christy Harrison)
- *The Full Bloom* (Zoë Bisbing, season 4, episode #75 with Da'Shaun L. Harrison)
- *Maintenance Phase* (Michael Hobbes and Aubrey Gordon)
- *Men Unscripted* (Aaron Flores)
- *My Black Body* (Jessica Wilson and Rawiyah Tariq)
- *She's All Fat* (Sophia Carter-Kahn)
- *Unsolicited: Fatties Talk Back* (Marquisele Mercedes, Caleb Luna, Bryan Guffey, Jordan Underwood, and Da'Shaun Harrison)

Instagram Content

- Aaron Flores, RDN (@aaronfloresrdn)
- adrienne maree brown (@adriennemareebrown)
- Alisha McCullough, LCMHC (@blackandembodied)
- Aubrey Gordon (@yrfatfriend)

ANTI-DIET AND BODY LIBERATION RESOURCES

- Body Reborn (@bodyreborn)
- Caleb Luna (@dr_chairbreaker)
- Center for Body Trust® (@center4bodytrust)
- Chrissy King (@iamchrissyking)
- Dalina Soto, RD, LDN (@your.latina.nutritionist)
- Evelyn Tribole, MS, RDN, CEDRD-S (@evelyntribole)
- FedUp Collective (@fedupcollective)
- Food Dignity Movement (@fooddignitymovement)
- Gloria Lucas (@nalgonapositivitypride)
- Hannah Fuhlendorf, MA, LPC (@hannahtalksbodies)
- Ilya Parker (@decolonizing_fitness)
- Jessamyn Stanley (@mynameisjessamyn)
- Jessica Wilson, MS, RD (@jessicawilson.msrd)
- Joy Cox, PhD (@Freshoutthecocoon)
- Katja Rowell, MD (@katjarowellmd)
- Marci Evans, RD (@marcird)
- Marquisele Mercedes (@fatmarquisele)
- Mount Sinai Hospital Eating Disorders Center (@mountsinaiewdp)
- Multi-Service Eating Disorders Association (@recoverwithmeda)
- Natalie Gutiérrez, LMFT (@nataliegutierrezlmft)
- Project Heal (@projectheal)
- Rachel (Rae) Estapa (@rachelestapa)
- Rachel Millner, PhD (@drrachelmilner)
- Ragen Chastain (@ragenchastain)
- Sand Chang, PhD (@heydrsand)
- Shana Minei Spence, MS, RDN, CDN (@thenutritiontea)
- Sonya Renee Taylor (@sonyareneetaylor)
- Virginia Sole-Smith (@v_solesmith)
- Whitney Trotter, RD (@whitneytrotter.rd)

References

Anderson, F., Sweezy, M., & Schwartz, R. C. (2017). *Internal Family Systems skills training manual: Trauma-informed treatment for anxiety, depression, PTSD & substance abuse*. PESI Publishing.

Angelou, M. (2014). *Rainbow in the cloud: The wisdom and spirit of Maya Angelou*. Random House.

Ayoola, E. (2023, February 27). We need to talk about eating disorders within the Black community. *Essence*. https://www.essence.com/health-and-wellness/eating-disorders-in-the-black-community

Chastain, R. (2023). The problem with weight stigma research. *Substack: Weight and Healthcare*. https://weightandhealthcare.substack.com/p/the-problem-with-weight-stigma-research

DeSteno, D. (2014). A feeling of control: How America can finally learn to deal with its impulses. *Pacific Standard Magazine*. https://psmag.com/social-justice/feeling-control-america-can-finally-learn-deal-impulses-self-regulation-89456

Dickens, L., & DeSteno, D. (2016). The grateful are patient: Heightened daily gratitude is associated with attenuated temporal discounting. *Emotion, 16*(4), 421–425. https://doi.org/10.1037/emo0000176

Ferguson, S. (2014). Privilege 101: A quick and dirty guide. *Everyday Feminism*. https://everydayfeminism.com/2014/09/what-is-privilege

Flegal, K. M. (2021). The obesity wars and the education of a researcher: A personal account. *Progress in Cardiovascular Diseases, 67*, 75–79. https://doi.org/10.1016/j.pcad.2021.06.009

Floyd, T. (2023). Creating access to IFS training and consultation for BIPOC therapists. In E. Redfern (Ed.), *Internal Family Systems therapy: Supervision and consultation* (pp. 78–93). Routledge.

Galmiche, M., Dechelotte, P., Lambert, G., & Tavolacci, M. P. (2019). Prevalence of eating disorders over the 2000–2018 period: A systematic literature review. *The American Journal of Clinical Nutrition, 109*(5), 1402–1413. https://doi.org/10.1093/ajcn/nqy342

Gay, R. (2017). *Hunger: A memoir of (my) body*. HarperCollins.

Gordon, A. (2023). *"You just need to lose weight": And 19 other myths about fat people*. Beacon Press.

Gou, Y., & Schwartz, M. W. (2023). How should we think about the unprecedented weight loss efficacy of incretin-mimetic drugs? *The Journal of Clinical Investigation, 133*(19), 1–3. https://doi.org/10.1172/JCI174597

Gutiérrez, N. Y. (2022). *The pain we carry: Healing from complex PTSD for people of color*. New Harbinger Publications.

Hagen, S. (2022, March 17). Sofie Hagen on the legacy of lockdown: I realised what the world feels like for thin people. *The Guardian*. https://www.theguardian.com/lifeandstyle/2022/mar/17/sofie-hagen-on-the-legacy-of-lockdown-i-realised-what-the-world-feels-like-for-thin-people

Haines, S. K. (2019). *The politics of trauma: Somatics, healing, and social justice*. North Atlantic Books.

Harrison, D. L. (2021). *Belly of the beast: The politics of anti-fatness as anti-Blackness*. North Atlantic Books.

Himmelstein, M. S., Incollingo Belsky, A. C., & Tomiyama, A. J. (2015). The weight of stigma: Cortisol reactivity to manipulated weight stigma. *Obesity, 23*(2), 368–374. https://doi.org/10.1002/oby.20959

Kaur, V. (2017, November). *3 lessons of revolutionary love in a time of rate* [Video]. TED Conferences. https://www.ted.com/talks/valarie_kaur_3_lessons_of_revolutionary_love_in_a_time_of_rage

Kidd, C., Palmeri, H., & Aslin, R. N. (2013). Rational snacking: Young children's decision-making on the marshmallow task is moderated by beliefs about environmental reliability. *Cognition, 126*(1), 109–114. https://doi.org/10.1016/j.cognition.2012.08.004

Kinavey, H., & Sturtevant, D. (2022). *Reclaiming body trust: A path to healing & liberation*. TarcherPerigee.

King, C. (2023). *The body liberation project: How understanding racism and diet culture helps cultivate joy and build collective freedom*. Tiny Reparations Books.

REFERENCES

Kochhar, R. (2023, March 1). The enduring grip of the gender pay gap. *Pew Research Center.* https://www.pewresearch.org/social-trends/2023/03/01/the-enduring-grip-of-the-gender-pay-gap/

Lee, K. M., Hunger, J. M., & Tomiyama, A. J. (2021). Weight stigma and health behaviors: Evidence from the Eating in America study. *International Journal of Obesity, 45,* 1499–1509. https://doi.org/10.1038/s41366-021-00814-5

Luna, C. (Host). (2023, June 18). Un/touchable (No. 15) [Audio podcast episode]. In *Unsolicited: Fatties Talk Back.* https://unsolicitedftb.libsyn.com/untouchable

Manne, K. (2024). *Unshrinking: How to face fatphobia.* Crown.

Matz, J. (2022). Unlearning weight stigma: The latest science on weight and trauma. *Psychotherapy Networker, 46*(1), 54–58.

Mercedes, M., & Kriete, M. (2023, May). *Anti-fatness in public health.* New England Public Health Training Center. https://www.nephtc.org/enrol/index.php?id=336

McConnell, S. (2020). *Somatic Internal Family Systems therapy: Awareness, breath, resonance, movement, and touch in practice.* North Atlantic Books.

McKinsey & Company. (2022). *Women in the Workplace 2022.* https://wiw-report.s3.amazonaws.com/Women_in_the_Workplace_2022.pdf

McMillan Cottom, T. (2023, October 9). Ozempic can't fix what our culture has broken. *The New York Times.* https://www.nytimes.com/2023/10/09/opinion/ozempic-obesity-fat-diabetes.html

Mischel, W. (1961). Father-absence and delay of gratification. *Journal of Abnormal and Social Psychology, 63*(1), 116–124. https://doi.org/10.1037/h0046877

Mischel, W., & Ebbesen, E. B. (1970). Attention in delay of gratification. *Journal of Personality and Social Psychology, 16*(2), 329–337. https://doi.org/10.1037/h0029815

Mischel, W., Ebbesen, E. B., & Raskoff Zeiss, A. (1972). Cognitive and attentional mechanisms in delay of gratification. *Journal of Personality and Social Psychology, 21*(2), 204–218. https://doi.org/10.1037/h0032198

Mischel, W., & Grusec, J. (1967). Waiting for rewards and punishments: Effects of time and probability on choice. *Journal of Personality and Social Psychology, 5*(1), 24–31. https://doi.org/10.1037/h0024180

Muldoon, C. (2022, August 23). Wellness vs. well-being: What's the difference? *WebMD Health Services.* https://www.webmdhealthservices .com/blog/wellness-vs-well-being-whats-the-difference

Nam, S., Jeon, S., Lee, S. J., Ash, G., Nelson, L. E., & Granger, D. A. (2022). Real-time racial discrimination, affective states, salivary cortisol and alpha-amylase in Black adults. *PLoS ONE, 17*(9), e0273081. https://doi.org/10 .1371/journal.pone.0273081

Pastor, M. (2013). *The unburdened internal system* [Online image]. https: //www.marielpastor.com/the-unburdened-system.

Pearl, R. L., Wadden, T. A., Hopkins, C. M., Shaw, J. A., Hayes, M. R., Bakizada, Z. M., Alfaris, N., Chao, A. M., Pinkasavage, E., Berkowitz, R. I., & Alamuddin, N. (2017). Association between weight bias internalization and metabolic syndrome among treatment-seeking individuals with obesity. *Obesity, 25,* 317–322. https://doi.org/10.1002 /oby.21716

Piran, N. (2017). *Journeys of embodiment at the intersection of body and culture: The developmental theory of embodiment.* Academic Press.

Piran, N. (2020, March 13). *Day 5: The five dimensions of embodiment* [Conference session]. Be Nourished Body Trust Summit 2020.

Robinson, E. R., & Sutin, A. R. (2017). Parents' perceptions of their children as overweight and children's weight concerns and weight gain. *Psychological Science, 28*(3), 320–329. https://doi.org/10.1177/0956797616682027

Roehling, P. V., Roehling, M. V., & Elluru, A. (2018). Size does matter: The impact of size on career. In A. M. Broadbridge & S. L. Fielden (Eds.), *Research handbook of diversity and careers* (pp. 105–115). Edward Elgar Publishing.

Satter, E. M. (1986). The feeding relationship. *Journal of the American Dietetic Association, 86*(3), 352–356. https://doi.org/10.1016/S0002 -8223(21)03940-7

Schlam, T. R., Wilson, N. L., Shoda, Y., Mischel, W., & Ayduk, O. (2013). Preschoolers' delay of gratification predicts their body mass 30 years later. *The Journal of Pediatrics, 162*(1), 90–93. https://doi.org/10.1016/j.jpeds .2012.06.049

REFERENCES

Schvey, N. A., Puhl, R. M., & Brownell, K. D. (2014). The stress of stigma: Exploring the effect of weight stigma on cortisol reactivity. *Psychosomatic Medicine, 76*(2), 156–162. https://doi.org/10.1097/PSY .0000000000000031

Schwartz, R. C. (1995). *Internal Family Systems therapy.* Guilford Press.

Schwartz, R. C. (2021). *No bad parts: Healing trauma and restoring wholeness with the Internal Family Systems model.* Sounds True Publications.

Schwartz, R. C., & Sweezy, M. (2020). *Internal Family Systems therapy* (2nd ed.). Guilford Press.

Shoda, Y., Mischel, W., & Peake, P. (1990). Predicting adolescent cognitive and self-regulatory competencies from preschool delay of gratification: Identifying diagnostic conditions. *Developmental Psychology, 26*(6), 978–986. https://doi.org/10.1037/0012-1649.26.6.978

Sinko, A. L. (2016). Legacy burdens. In M. Sweezy & E. L. Ziskind (Eds.), *Innovations and elaborations in Internal Family Systems therapy* (pp. 164–178). Routledge.

Strings, S. (2019). *Fearing the Black body: The racial origins of fat phobia.* New York University Press.

Small, C. (2021). Eating because we're hungry or because something's eating us? In C. Small & M. Fuller (Eds.), *Treating Black women with eating disorders: A clinician's guide* (pp. 13–32). Routledge.

Sole-Smith, V. (2023). *Fat talk: Parenting in the age of diet culture.* Henry Holt and Company.

Sowell, N., Sweezy, M., & Schwartz, R. C. (in press). *Internal Family Systems therapy for physical health and illness: Healing the underlying stress, shame, and trauma.* PESI Publishing.

Sutin, A. R., Rust, G., Robinson, E., Daly, M., & Terracciano, A. (2017). Parental perception of child weight and inflammation: Perceived overweight is associated with higher child C-reactive protein. *Biological Psychology, 130*, 50–53. https://doi.org/10.1016/j.biopsycho.2017.10.004

Sykes, C. (2016). An IFS lens on addiction: Compassion for extreme parts. In M. Sweezy & E. L. Ziskind (Eds.), *Innovations and elaborations in Internal Family Systems therapy* (pp. 29–48). Routledge.

Sykes, C., Sweezy, M., & Schwartz, R. C. (2023). *Internal Family Systems therapy for addictions: Trauma-informed, compassion-based interventions for substance use, eating, gambling and more.* PESI Publishing.

Taylor, S. R. (2018). *The body is not an apology: The power of radical self-love.* Berrett-Koehler Publishing.

Taylor, S. R. [@sonyareneetaylor]. (2021, January 15). *Posted @withregram @thebodyisnotanapology In @SonyaReneeTaylor's video posted this morning, she analyzes current debates about whether Trump would be able to.* [Photograph]. Instagram. https://www.instagram.com/p/CKE8yL6A8Ev/?hl=en

Thompson, B. W. (1994). *A hunger so wide and so deep: American women speak out on eating problems.* University Of Minnesota Press.

Tomiyama, A. J., Carr, D., Granberg, E. M., Major, B., Robinson, E., Sutin, A. R., & Brewis, A. (2018). How and why weight stigma drives the "obesity epidemic" and harms health. *BMC Medicine, 16*(123). https://doi.org/10.1186/s12916-018-1116-5

Tribole, E. [@evelyntribole]. (2019, June 7). *A systematic review found that the prevalence of eating disorders doubled from 3.5% for the 2000–2006 period, to 7.8%* [Photograph]. Instagram. https://www.instagram.com/p/ByZoWK7FuFT/

Tribole, E., & Resch, E. (2020). *Intuitive Eating: A revolutionary anti-diet approach* (4th ed.). St. Martin's Essentials.

Tovar, V. (2017, October 19). Take the cake: The 3 levels of fatphobia. *Ravishly.* https://ravishly.com/3-levels-of-fatphobia

Watts, T. W., Duncan, G. J., & Quan, H. (2018). Revisiting the marshmallow test: A conceptual replication investigating links between early delay of gratification and later outcomes. *Psychological Science, 29*(7), 1159–1177. https://doi.org/10.1177/0956797618761661

Wilson, J. (2023). *It's always been ours: Rewriting the story of Black women's bodies.* Hachette Go.

Yurkevich, V. (2023, May 11). New York City passes bill banning weight discrimination. *CNN Business.* https://www.cnn.com/2023/05/11/business/new-york-weight-discrimination/index.html

Acknowledgments

This book is based on what I've learned about myself and my clients over the past thirty years. I wish that I had known about this powerful way of healing from the outset of my career as a psychologist. To those clients who allowed me to share their experiences here, thank you for your courage and generosity. I am so grateful to you.

My social location as a cisgender, affluent White woman gives me access that isn't available to many people. I have struggled with the question of whether to share my perspective when there are others whose voices deserve to be heard and promoted. My primary goal in writing this book is to use what I've learned to open the hearts and minds of other White people to the racism and other oppressive systems that underlie the dieting and wellness industries. In this regard, I want to acknowledge Niva Piran, Aubrey Gordon, Virginia Sole-Smith, Hilary Kinavey, Dana Sturtevant, Ragen Chastain, Christy Harrison, and others whose work has been instrumental to my learning about the pernicious underpinnings of diet and wellness culture. Their writing and other offerings introduced me to the BIPOC clinicians and activists who have continued the body liberation work of activists in the late 1960s and early 1970s. Among others, Sonya Renee Taylor, Marquisele Mercedes, Da'Shaun L. Harrison, adrienne maree brown, Sabrina Strings, Jessica Wilson, and Caleb Luna have been particularly impactful in expanding my awareness of anti-fat and other body-related bias. Thank you for making your wisdom and knowledge accessible. Where possible, I strive to acknowledge your work and to support you.

To my friends, family, and colleagues who have heard about this book long enough to wonder if this is my second book, thank you for your continued interest and support. A few people deserve special mention. Elizabeth Doyne's steady encouragement saw me through many periods of serious self-doubt and inertia. Her wise input and openness to exploring her own biases were invaluable. Kay Gardner and Sarah Stewart were similarly helpful in supporting this project and conveying their belief in its value. I am deeply grateful to Veronique Mead and Meg Gehman for providing me with feedback on initial drafts of this book and to Debra Rosenzweig, Jen Nield, Griet Op de Beeck, and Joanne Gaffney-Livingstone for their careful reading of the final draft. Their input greatly improved the final version.

To Jane Gerhard, my wise, skillful, and irreverent editor, who helped me identify my love for adjectives in groups of three (among other things), thank you for your unwavering and generous support and friendship.

To Jenessa Jackson, my PESI editor, who added to my learning about writing and, especially, punctuation. Thank you for your helpful revisions. I appreciate Linda Jackson, my PESI publisher, for her steadfast patience and positive outlook throughout this process.

To Richard Schwartz, whose model has brought so much healing to me and to so many, thank you for your love and support. I am so fortunate to have you as my partner in life and to join you in bringing this tremendously healing approach to the world.

And, finally, to Sadie and Phoebe, who sat beside me through countless drafts.

About the Author

Jeanne Catanzaro, PhD, is a clinical psychologist who has specialized in treating eating disorders and trauma for the past twenty-five years. She trained in psychodynamic psychotherapy, Somatic Experiencing®, and eye movement desensitization and reprocessing (EMDR) before discovering the Internal Family Systems (IFS) model. An approved IFS consultant, she served as the director of a day treatment program for eating disorders for two years. She has written three chapters on using IFS to treat eating disorders, one in *Innovations and Elaborations in Internal Family Systems Therapy* (2016), another in *Trauma-Informed Approaches to Eating Disorders* (2018), and a third in *Internal Family Systems Therapy Supervision and Consultation* (2022). For the past ten years, she's been focused on healing eating issues across the spectrum. This book is an outgrowth of her interest in helping people heal the cultural legacy burdens that disrupt their Self-led relationships with their bodies.

About the Illustrator

Sacha Mardou is a British cartoonist and graphic novelist who now makes a home in St. Louis, Missouri. Her graphic memoir *Past Tense: Facing Family Secrets and Finding Myself in Therapy* (Avery Press, 2024) is an account of her emotional healing journey using IFS therapy. Find her online @mardou_draws (Instagram), @sachamardou (Facebook), and on her website, https://ifscomics.com.